COOK
SHARE
EAT
VEGAN

COOK
SHARE
EAT
VEGAN

DELICIOUS PLANT-BASED RECIPES FOR EVERYONE
ÁINE CARLIN

MITCHELL BEAZLEY

CONTENTS

MY VEGAN KITCHEN

For as long as I can remember the kitchen has been the social focal point of any place I have ever called home—whether the Irish childhood home that gave me Sunday dinners and creamy rice puddings, the London one I briefly shared with friends in my twenties (with its array of varying tastes and preferences), or the current place in Penzance, in the south-west of England, that my husband and I have lovingly cultivated. Each has shown me the power food possesses in bringing us together, no matter what cultural background we may come from, or indeed what dietary requirements we might have. For me, veganism has opened so many doors and has brought me so much joy and inner peace, it makes sense that I want to share it with my friends and family. Nothing brings me more happiness than creating an abundance of wholesome, seasonal food that will perfectly set the stage for any gathering, no matter how fancy or humble.

Of course, I like to treat every meal as an event, which is why the dishes in this book are suitable for a variety of occasions, even if those occasions happen to involve being curled up on the couch on a gloomy Wednesday with only one person to feed—yourself. You could say my raison d'etre is to ensure food (and the cooking thereof) is both straightforward and delicious in equal measure. I've long since held the belief that food created under any sort of duress (self-inflicted or otherwise) never tastes quite as good as a dish made with ease and love. And while the odd recipe might require a little more effort, you can rest assured that nothing in this book is beyond even the most nervous cook's capabilities.

Keeping things simple means that you'll find similar ingredients, sauces, dressings, and food combinations rearing their familiar heads at various points throughout the chapters of this book. There are many practical reasons for having staples at the heart of your repertoire—I find it gives me the ability to improvise freely around what I like to call my "fundamental foodie structure." My "Goes-With-Everything" Tahini Sauce (see page 151) is a perfect example: due to its endless versatility, I find myself tweaking it to accompany both sweet and savory dishes on a regular basis, without it ever feeling predictable or dull. Likewise, you'll notice I have a thing for black beans and avocado (see the Chimichangas on page 76 or my crazy good Baked Potato Nachos on page 156 for proof), and try as I might to break this addiction, somehow I still gravitate to this naturally delicious duo and never once regret it.

I like to think that many of my recipes are simply jumping-off points for people who are seeking a little encouragement when it comes to plant-based cooking. My aim is always to sway the focus away from the "vegan" tagline and instead bring the food itself to the fore. Creating beautiful, colorful, nutritious food that never fails to raise an approving smile is absolutely at the core of my cooking. And yes, it just happens to be vegan too.

THE BASICS

While veganism is making its way to the mainstream that doesn't mean there aren't still a few helpful tips and tricks that can make your life a little easier. So before you get cracking with the recipes, these are the basics that need covering.

HOW AND WHY TO SOAK NUTS

You'll notice that nuts play a vital role in my plant-based lifestyle, and rightly so. Not only are they important for a balanced, nutritious diet, providing us with essential fats and various amounts of protein and calcium, but they also happen to be fabulously versatile. To get the best out of your nuts you'll want to soak them beforehand—simply place your nuts in a bowl and pour over enough filtered water to completely cover them. Don't panic about this, I simply mean water from a filter jug or filter faucet, not bottled water, but if you don't have a water filter then regular water will do.

I usually soak my nuts overnight but certain types are more susceptible to "turning"—for example, cashews can become slimy if left to soak for too long, so I try to use those within an 8-hour period or thereabouts. It goes without saying that the harder the nut the longer the soak, so almonds, macadamias, and Brazil nuts really do benefit from being left for a few extra hours. Once you've finished soaking, simply drain the nuts and rinse them under cold running water before using them as you like.

> QUICK SOAK TIP! At a pinch you can cover your nuts with freshly boiled water and set them aside for 30 minutes. This soak won't be quite as effective but it will still soften the nuts enough to make them easier to blend.

PLANT MILKS

I make a variety of plant milks on a weekly rotation, using the same basic recipe. For milks I've settled on the three-to-one ratio—that means three parts liquid to one part nut. You could make the nuts stretch a little farther by opting for a four-to-one ratio (which will still be very creamy and almost akin to the consistency of lowfat milk) but I just adore the rich deliciousness of slightly thicker plant milks. These also tend to work much better in coffee and tea. Speaking of which, you'll soon notice that some plant milks tend to curdle more than others in hot drinks, but I've never had an issue with oat milk, which makes for a particularly wonderful creamer. Temperature usually plays a role in why plant milks curdle so I find it helps to let the coffee or tea cool slightly first, as well as heating the milk a little before using. These are things you'll soon get the hang of, so even if it fails once you'll eventually find the knack.

Because there's no need to soak oats that usually puts oat milk at the top of the pile for me, but I also adore almond milk, which definitely comes a very close second. Cashew milk is a favorite for many because it doesn't necessarily need straining, although I do so anyway because I like my milks super-smooth. And when it comes to straining, nut-milk bags can be obtained easily online and are specifically designed for straining nut milks without the problem of using a cheesecloth (though they do exactly the same job). Plant milks do sometimes separate in the refrigerator (it's normal, don't panic) so always give them a good shake before using. It's also wise to invest in a couple of glass bottles—I favor the traditional Weck brand but any BPA-free bottle will suffice. Enough babble, onto the milk …

BASIC PLANT MILK RECIPE
MAKES APPROX. 3 CUPS

generous ¾ cup soaked and drained nuts
   (*see* opposite) or unsoaked rolled oats
3 cups filtered water

1. Place the nuts (or oats) and water in a blender and blend for up to 1 minute until smooth. A high-speed blender will produce smoother results, but a regular blender is fine.

2. Strain through a nut-milk bag or some cheesecloth, to collect any unwanted pulp.
3. Transfer to a sterilized glass bottle and refrigerate for up to 4 days.

> FLAVOR TIP! If you want to flavor your nut milk, the possibilities are endless. From time to time I like adding a pinch of pink Himalayan salt, a little vanilla extract or maple syrup or a touch of ground cinnamon.

DAIRY-FREE CREAMS

Creams are a mainstay in my kitchen, in both savory and sweet dishes. How creamy you require them to be will be reflected in the amount of liquid added—sour cream will need slightly more water than, say, cream for a cheesecake. Once you've achieved the desired consistency, these creams become a great backdrop for an array of flavors, such as the chipotle sour cream that accompanies my Sweet Potato Hash Browns (*see* page 86). Creamy fillings for dairy-free desserts such as the Matcha & Lime Pie (*see* page 192) can also be easily altered to suit: if you're not so keen on citrus, for example, then add a heaping tablespoon of raw cacao to the mix instead for a wonderfully rich alternative. Here are a few of my essential everyday recipes:

CASHEW SOUR CREAM
MAKES APPROX. 1 CUP

I typically use this cashew cream recipe as a base, adding various spices and pastes to create an entirely different vibe each time. It is wonderfully versatile and a great one to have up your sleeve. For a sweeter version, omit the cider vinegar.

1¼ cups soaked cashews (*see* page 8), drained
½ cup filtered water
juice of ½ lemon
1 teaspoon cider vinegar
½ teaspoon sea salt flakes

Place everything in a blender and blend until smooth, scraping down the sides from time to time. With plant creams it is crucial you get them as smooth as possible—they will go through several stages before they get there, so persevere until you reach the desired consistency. Check for seasoning and refrigerate until needed.

ALMOND POURING CREAM
MAKES APPROX. 1½ CUPS

¾ cup soaked blanched almonds (*see* page 8), drained
generous 1 cup filtered water, plus extra if necessary
3 tablespoons maple syrup
1 teaspoon vanilla extract
pinch of sea salt flakes

Add everything to a blender and blend until you achieved a pouring (light cream) consistency, adding a little more water if necessary.

MACADAMIA CREAM
MAKES APPROX. ¾ CUP

Macadamia cream can be used to great effect in both sweet and savory dishes. Once blended it becomes light and fluffy and is delicate enough to absorb a variety of flavors. For savory creams I stick to brighter notes by adding a little lemon or lime juice (cashew cream is much more suited to robust flavors) and I usually avoid adding any sort of vinegar. If I want to sweeten things up I add agave nectar or maple syrup (and a touch of natural extract such as lemon or vanilla) but I try not to overdo it because macadamias have a wonderful natural sweetness that shouldn't be overshadowed. They might be pricey, but for an occasional treat they are worth the investment.

generous ¾ cup macadamias, soaked
5 tablespoons filtered water, plus extra if necessary
¼ teaspoon sea salt flakes

Add everything to a blender and blend, scraping down the sides from time to time and adding a splash or two more water if necessary, until light and fluffy.

HOW TO TOAST NUTS & SEEDS

In order to get the best out of nuts, you sometimes have to give them a little encouragement in the oven or on the stove. It's also the easiest way to remove those stubborn skins. Once you remove the nuts from the heat, place them in a clean dish towel and rub vigorously—the skins should come off effortlessly.

For a more even toasting—even for delicate nuts such as slivered almonds or coconut flakes—the oven works best. I arrange the nuts on a baking sheet in an even layer and toast them in an oven preheated to 400°F for 10 to 15 minutes, or until golden and crunchy, shaking the sheet occasionally and keeping an eye on them to ensure they don't burn (this can happen quickly). When toasting nuts on the stove I place them in a dry pan set over medium heat and toast them for up to 5 minutes, tossing them lightly.

A NOTE ON SUGARS

I don't discriminate when it comes to sugar. While on a daily basis I try to stick to the unrefined variety, I see no harm in using superfine, granulated, or light brown sugar in baking as and when needed—my Vegan Pavlova (*see* page 226) simply doesn't work with liquid sweeteners. I also try not to place too much (if any) guilt on such things because, really, life's too short. If it's consumed in moderation then I don't think we should be overly concerned.

A NOTE ON FLOURS

I use a wide variety of flours in my recipes, everything from buckwheat through to spelt, rye, rice, and gram (chickpea)—and, yes, even good old regular white flour, which you will see crop up in a number of dishes here and there. If you have a gluten-intolerance issue then substitute it with a suitable alternative (there are a wide variety now on the market) but I'm perfectly happy to use and eat all flours, even those now deemed "unhealthy" by some. I always endeavor to buy organic and usually make my baked goods in small batches, so I never feel as if I'm overdoing it on the flour front anyway. After all, bread is life—or at least in my world it is.

LET'S TALK ABOUT TOFU

I want to address any queries or reservations you might have about tofu right away—while I understand that you might have put bean curd firmly in the "bleurgh" category, I'm here to gently right those wrongs and put it back on the menu. Tofu will readily absorb any flavors you throw at it. The longer you marinate it, the more flavorful it will become—just remember to season, season, season! Then it's just a matter of cooking it to your liking and adding it to your favorite dish.

To keep things simple there are, generally speaking, two main varieties of tofu on the market—firm and silken. Firm tofu is typically reserved for savory dishes and really benefits from being "pressed." Simply drain the tofu block and pat it dry before placing it in a shallow bowl. Put a plate on top and weigh it down with several cans of tomatoes, beans, or similar, then set it aside for at least 1 hour so the tofu can release any remaining liquid it might be retaining. Drain it again and refrigerate until needed before either frying, baking, marinating, or scrambling.

Silken tofu has a much more jellylike texture and doesn't really stand up to frying or baking (and whatever you do, don't throw it into a stew). It comes into its own when blended, however, making a terrific base for egg-free mayo (*see* page 172). It is also positively mind-blowing when used in desserts—for proof check out my Chocolate Orange Pots (*see* page 200).

WHAT'S IN MY PANTRY?

What appears on my shopping list time and time again, I hear you ask? I've been cultivating this selection for years and add to it periodically, but these are pretty much my staples. I've divided the list into handy categories so you can see at a glance what I reach for on a regular basis. As much as I try to buy local, I do frequent grocery stores and the odd health-food store as well.

OILS & BUTTERS

Chili oil
Coconut oil
Garlic oil
Hazelnut oil
Olive oil (extra virgin and regular)
Sesame oil (toasted and regular)
Truffle oil
Coconut butter
Dairy-free margarine
Vegetable shortening

GRAINS

Bulgur wheat
Couscous
Freekeh
Millet
Pearl barley
Quinoa (all varieties)
Rice (basmati, brown, risotto, and wild)
Spelt

BEANS & LEGUMES

Black beans
Black-eyed peas
Cannellini beans
Chickpeas
Kidney beans
Lentils (green, red, Puy, and Beluga)
Lima beans
Yellow split peas

SAUCES, POWDERS, VINEGARS & PASTES

Extracts (vanilla, lemon, orange, coffee, and almond)
Mustard (Dijon, whole-grain, and English)
Nutritional yeast
Orange blossom water
Rose water
Sriracha chili sauce
Tamari and soy sauce
Thai sweet chili sauce
Chlorella powder
Maca powder
Matcha powder
Raw cacao powder and cocoa
Cider vinegar
Red wine vinegar
Rice mirin
Chipotle paste
Harissa paste
Miso paste (both sweet and dark)
Vegan Thai curry paste (both red and green)

HERBS & SPICES

Bay leaves
Chives
Cilantro
Dill
Mint
Flat-leaf parsley
Rosemary
Tarragon
Thyme

Cardamom pods
Cloves
Dried chili flakes
Dried oregano
Garam masala
Ground cinnamon
Ground coriander
Ground cumin
Ground turmeric
Kaffir lime leaves
Nutmeg
Peppercorns
Ras el hanout
Salt (fine and coarse sea salt and pink Himalayan)
Smoked paprika
Star anise
Za'atar

NUTS, SEEDS & DRIED FRUITS

Almonds (both slivered and whole)
Brazil nuts
Cashews
Peanuts (unsalted)
Pecans
Pistachios
Walnuts
Chia
Flaxseed
Pumpkin seeds
Sunflower seeds
Dates (medjool)
Dried apricots
Dried berries
Dried mulberries
Raisins

JARRED & CANNED GOODS

Canned tomatoes (plum, chopped, strained, and puree)
Coconut cream
Coconut milk
Corn
Dairy-free pesto
Nut butters (peanut, almond, and cashew)
Tahini

FRESH PRODUCE

Apples
Bananas
Lemons and limes
Mangoes
Nectarines
Oranges
Pears
Butternut squash
Chili
Eggplant
Garlic
Ginger
Kale (including Tuscan kale)
Leeks
Mushrooms
Onions
Potatoes (sweet and regular)
Spinach
Zucchini

FOOD FOR FRIENDS

LAID-BACK BRUNCH

Brunch is where it's at right now, maybe because the pressure seems to be off earlier in the day or maybe it's because I'm typically more chilled first thing. People generally aren't expecting a gargantuan meal at 11 a.m. but I still like to keep them satisfied. My Lemon Chia Pudding is a great way to kick off proceedings because it enlivens the palate and isn't too heavy. Best of all it can be made in advance, which means you can focus on the main event. Because we've started off sweet, I like to graduate to something savory like my Corn Fritters, which are surprisingly easy to make and also gluten free. Obviously I'll have a pot of tea or coffee on the go but I also like to fill small tumblers with my Super Green Smoothie. I normally squeeze it through a nut-milk bag and refrigerate it before serving, so it's nicely chilled.

> **Lemon Chia Pudding with a Warm Blackberry Compote & Toasted Coconut (***see* **page 38)**
> **Corn Fritters with Quick-Pickled Carrot (***see* **page 64)**
> **Super Green Smoothie (***see* **page 45)**

LIGHT LUNCH

I love having friends over for lunch and Romaine Lettuce Wraps are perfect for getting my guests involved—I simply lay everything out on the table and let them help themselves. I pop some Wasabi-Dusted Popcorn on the table while I'm prepping, as it's just enough to tide people over until we eat. The Matcha & Lime Pie is so zesty and fresh that most people won't refuse a slice to round off what is a light but satisfying lunch.

> **Wasabi-Dusted Popcorn (***see* **page 114)**
> **Romaine Lettuce Wraps with Spicy Coconut Chickpeas & Zesty Cauli-Rice (***see* **page 54)**
> **Matcha & Lime Pie with Macerated Strawberries (***see* **page 192)**

INFORMAL DINNER

Informal gatherings are the crux of my social scene. I don't always play host, but when my friends do happen to come over I tend to go all out—without disintegrating into a kitchen-induced meltdown, of course. This Salsa-Style Panzanella Salad is the perfect way to start proceedings, because it gets people sharing right off the bat and sets the tone for the evening. The Polenta Pizza is also a bit of a tear and share affair, brilliantly complemented by my absolute new favorite side dish, Crispy Potato Fries with a Parsley & Almond Sauce. Those things will fly off the plate, so you best make a double batch. When it comes to the next course, I offer up something savory for the "cheese heads" with my Dill-Coated Cashew Cheese as well as a refreshing palate cleanser in the form of my Grapefruit, Gin & Sage Granita, both of which can be made in advance, leaving you to enjoy the party. Granted this is more of a summer shindig menu than a cozy winter one, but it's a dinner party that everyone will delight in.

> **Salsa-Style Panzanella Salad with Griddled Nectarines** (*see* page 50)
> **Polenta Pizza with Spinach & Roasted Squash** (*see* page 68)
> **Crispy Potato Fries with a Parsley & Almond Sauce** (*see* page 146)
> **Dill-Coated Cashew Cheese with Homemade "Nut-Pulp" Crackers** (*see* page 150)
> **Grapefruit, Gin & Sage Granita** (*see* page 210)

WINTER WARMER GATHERING

The festive season brings out the best in us, which is probably why we ramp up the socializing to extra-enthusiastic levels. As much as I love a party, the thought of catering them sometimes makes me break out in a sweat—I often think a halfway house between a formal dinner party and a casual gathering is where I feel most comfortable. This menu reflects my need to know exactly how many I will be feeding while still ensuring the meal is perfectly balanced and, of course, fun! I always like to offer people something to nibble on when they first arrive and this Beluga Lentil & Black Olive Dip works well as an intro. Next up are small warming bowls of Chestnut & Miso Soup served ahead of the main event, which in this case is Celeriac Steaks with a Mushroom Stroganoff Sauce, accompanied by a Massaged Kale & Toasted Walnut Salad. I like to wind things down with a fruit-based dessert like my Mulled Poached Pears—sweet enough to satisfy that nagging sweet tooth but light enough not to overwhelm. Interspersed with glasses of red wine, this menu is a winter warmer to remember.

> **Beluga Lentil & Black Olive Dip** (*see* page 169)
> **Chestnut & Miso Soup with Crunchy Chickpea Croutons** (*see* page 132)
> **Celeriac Steaks with a Mushroom Stroganoff Sauce** (*see* page 166)
> **Massaged Kale & Toasted Walnut Salad with Roasted Celeriac & Persimmon** (*see* page 142)
> **Mulled Poached Pears with a Silky Lemon & Thyme Cashew Cream** (*see* page 202)

ZESTY

CRISPY TOFU SALAD

with a zingy yuzu & miso dressing

SERVES 2

Tofu has a bad reputation, yet while many people think of it as a bland meat imposter, the reality couldn't be further from the truth. Consumed in Asia for centuries, it's a terrific source of protein that absorbs pretty much whatever you throw at it—or, in this particular case, toss it in. Yuzu is a lip-puckeringly sour but fragrant citrus fruit, the juice of which makes for a superb salad dressing. I like to balance out the intense sour notes here with a good dose of smoky sweetness from the maple syrup and some freshness in the form of lime, which helps to make this warm tofu salad something of an unexpected winner.

7 oz mixed salad greens
1 carrot, sliced into ribbons
1 zucchini, sliced into ribbons
1 persimmon, peeled and sliced
2 tablespoons cornstarch
grated zest of 1 lemon
¼ teaspoon sea salt flakes
¼ teaspoon black pepper
9 oz firm tofu, cut into bite-sized cubes
½ tablespoon peanut oil
1 teaspoon toasted sesame oil
1 tablespoon poppy seeds

2 scallions, chopped
lime slices, to garnish

Zingy yuzu & miso dressing
½ tablespoon yuzu juice
½ tablespoon sweet white miso paste
1 thumb-sized piece of fresh ginger root,
    peeled and minced
juice of ½ lime
1 tablespoon maple syrup

1. To make the dressing, vigorously whisk the ingredients together in a large bowl along with a splash of water to combine. Set aside until needed.

2. Place the salad greens, carrot, and zucchini ribbons and persimmon slices in a large bowl.

3. Combine the cornstarch with the lemon zest and salt and pepper in a bowl. Add the tofu cubes and toss lightly to coat.

4. Heat the peanut and sesame oils in a skillet over medium to high heat. Add the tofu to the pan and fry for 5 to 7 minutes, or until golden, tossing the pan from time to time to ensure all sides are crispy.

5. Tip the crispy tofu pieces into the dressing and toss to coat. Add the tofu to the salad bowl and pour over the remaining dressing. Sprinkle over the poppy seeds and chopped scallion and garnish with a few slices of lime.

ROASTED BEET, FENNEL & ORANGE SALAD

with a maple & orange dressing

SERVES 4

I often return to this classic combination of ingredients and each time I tweak and update it, I feel like I'm getting closer to the perfect salad. This version is a current favorite and looks especially beautiful when plated up. The roasted oranges almost melt in your mouth and are a great contrast to the fennel and beet, which both bring a robust earthiness to proceedings. Of course, no great salad is complete without a dressing and this maple and orange offering is one I perennially covet. This salad is best enjoyed at room temperature, so you can easily make it ahead of time knowing that it's happily marinating in all those wonderful juices, ready to be served.

4 beets, peeled and cut into wedges	Maple & orange dressing
3 large oranges	**1 tablespoon Dijon mustard**
2 tablespoons olive oil	**1 tablespoon cider vinegar**
2 fennel bulbs, cut into wedges	**2 tablespoons hazelnut oil**
¼ cup toasted hazelnuts	**½ tablespoon maple syrup**
small handful of dill	**juice of ½ orange**
sea salt flakes and black pepper	**sea salt flakes and black pepper**

1. Preheat the oven to 475°F.

2. Arrange the beet wedges on a baking sheet, add the grated zest and juice of half an orange, and 1 tablespoon of the olive oil, season well, and toss to combine. Cover with foil and roast for 40 minutes, then uncover and roast for another 5 to 10 minutes, shaking the sheet from time to time, until tender. Remove from the oven, season again, and squeeze over another 2 tablespoons or so of orange juice.

3. Meanwhile, place the fennel wedges in a baking dish, toss in the rest of the olive oil, season, and roast for 25 minutes, shaking the dish occasionally.

4. Cut the peel and rind off the remaining oranges and slice into thick circles. Add them to the fennel dish and roast for another 10 to 15 minutes, until caramelized.

5. To make the dressing, place all the ingredients in a bowl and whisk vigorously to combine. Season to taste.

6. Arrange the roasted beet, fennel, and orange pieces on a shallow plate or platter. Drizzle over the maple orange dressing and sprinkle over the toasted hazelnuts and dill just before serving.

PEA & ARUGULA CHICKPEA FLOUR PANCAKE

MAKES 2 LARGE PANCAKES

I was seriously tempted to dub this an "egg-free omelet," given its ability to replicate that one-time mainstay of my weekly menu so freakishly well. Instead I opted for the somewhat less polarizing title of "pancake" … although it does produce a very eggy-looking one of these. Vibrant yellow in color and packed full of peas (and therefore protein), this little number has become something of a personal favorite mainly thanks to its endless versatility. If you'd rather not include the peas in your batter rest assured, it will still be fabulous. Getting this pancake thin might take a bit of practice but it's definitely a skill worth adding to your expanding vegan repertoire.

¼ cup frozen peas
½ cup gram (chickpea) flour
1 tablespoon flaxseed meal
1 tablespoon nutritional yeast
½ teaspoon baking powder
½ teaspoon ground turmeric
juice of ½ lemon
½ cup water
1 heaping tablespoon chopped cilantro, plus
    extra to garnish

½ tablespoon coconut oil
2½ oz arugula leaves, plus extra to garnish
sea salt flakes and black pepper

Creamy coconut dressing
4 heaping tablespoons coconut yogurt
grated zest and juice of ½ lemon
1 tablespoon chopped cilantro
1 tablespoon chopped mint
sea salt flakes and black pepper

1. Place the peas in a small bowl and cover with freshly boiled water to defrost.

2. To make the coconut dressing, whisk the ingredients together in a small bowl until combined. Season to taste and refrigerate until needed.

3. Sift the gram flour into a mixing bowl. Add the flaxseed meal, yeast, baking powder, and turmeric and season with salt and pepper. Whisk to combine.

4. Make a well in the center of the flour, add the lemon juice and measured water, and whisk to form a batter.

5. Drain the peas and add to the batter along with the chopped cilantro. Stir to combine and set aside for 10 minutes to settle.

6. Set a crêpe pan or skillet over medium heat and brush it with the coconut oil. Ladle in half the batter and, using a spatula, push it to the edges of the pan—you want to get the pancake as thin as possible without it breaking. Cook for 5 to 7 minutes until the pancake is cooked through (you won't need to flip it).

7. Add half the arugula and dressing to the center of the pancake and ease it out onto a plate, using the pan to help gently fold it over. Repeat with the remaining batter. Serve the pancakes garnished with a little extra chopped cilantro, arugula and dressing.

SWEET POTATO GRATIN

with a panko lemon crumb

SERVES 4

I dread to think how many sweet potatoes I consume in any given week. Boiled, steamed, roasted, or fried, to me they are almost a food group in themselves and one that I never tire of experimenting with. This easy gratin dish might sound indulgent but it's actually a pretty healthy alternative to its dairy-laden counterpart, and the flaky, Japanese-style panko breadcrumbs make for a deliciously crunchy topping. A dauphinoise in essence, it's always sure to impress—whether you're hosting a formal dinner party or creating a casual lunch scenario. In my opinion it works for any food-centered occasion and is yet another string to add to your sweet potato-loving bow.

1 teaspoon coconut oil
2 large sweet potatoes, peeled, halved, and
    sliced into ½ inch thick pieces
4 teaspoons za'atar
1¼ cups soy cream (or oat cream or coconut
    milk)
1 cup panko bread crumbs
grated zest of 1 lemon
sea salt flakes and black pepper

1. Preheat the oven to 425°F. Grease a 12 x 8 inch ovenproof dish with the coconut oil.

2. Arrange the sweet potato pieces in the prepared dish in an even overlapping layer until the bottom is completely covered. Season with salt and pepper and sprinkle over 1 teaspoon of the za'atar, then pour over 7 tablespoons of the soy cream. Repeat the layers in the same fashion twice more for a total of 3 layers, ensuring all the sweet potato has been used and being sure to set aside 1 teaspoon of the za'atar.

3. Cover the gratin with lightly greased aluminum foil and bake for 50 minutes.

4. Meanwhile, combine the bread crumbs, lemon zest, and remaining za'atar in a bowl and season generously with salt and pepper.

5. Sprinkle the bread crumb mix over the gratin and bake for another 15 to 20 minutes until golden. Serve immediately.

CRISPY CINNAMON POTATO TACOS

with a lime & jalapeño sour cream

SERVES 4 TO 6

There are few things in life that give me more pleasure than tacos. With endless filling possibilities, wrapped in either crispy or soft tortillas (both have their virtues), they are the food equivalent of "one-size-fits-all." I've never met a person who doesn't relish wrapping their lips around one and if I ever did, I'm fairly certain we would not get along. If you're seeking a fail-safe dinner party hit then these crispy cinnamon potatoes—my current favorite taco incarnation—are most likely it, though I guarantee most questions will be about the lime and jalapeño sour cream, which is borderline life-changing.

1¾ lb salad potatoes, halved lengthwise and
  cut into ¼ inch thick slices
1½ teaspoons ground cinnamon, plus extra
  to serve
½ teaspoon cumin seeds
¼ teaspoon ground coriander
1 tablespoon maple syrup
3 tablespoons olive or canola oil
large handful of cilantro, coarsely chopped
grated zest of 1 lime
sea salt flakes and black pepper

Lime & jalapeño sour cream
1¼ cups cashews, soaked and drained
  (*see* page 8)
7 tablespoons water
grated zest and juice of 1 lime
1 teaspoon cider vinegar

1 tablespoon pickled jalapeños
sea salt flakes and black pepper

Corn & radish salsa
¾ cup corn kernels, preferably raw
4 radishes, finely chopped
1 celery stalk, finely chopped
2 scallions, finely chopped
1 green chile, finely chopped
grated zest and juice of 1 lime
1 tablespoon coarsely chopped flat-leaf parsley
1 tablespoon coarsely chopped dill
sea salt flakes and black pepper

To serve
10 to 12 taco-sized tortillas
7 oz arugula leaves
lime juice

1.   Preheat the oven to 425°F.

2.   To make the sour cream, place the cashews in a blender with the measured water, lime juice, vinegar, and jalapeños. Season and blend for at least 10 minutes, or until completely smooth. Scrape down the sides with a spatula every few minutes, bearing in mind that the cream will go through several stages until you achieve the desired smooth consistency. Transfer to a bowl and refrigerate until needed.

3.   Place the potatoes in an ovenproof dish and sprinkle over the cinnamon, cumin, and coriander, then drizzle with the maple syrup and 2 tablespoons of the oil. Season generously and toss to combine. Roast in the oven for 35 to 40, minutes or until golden and crisp, shaking the pan from time to time. Remove from the oven, season, and toss through the chopped cilantro and lime zest.

4. To make the salsa, place the corn kernels in a large bowl with the chopped radish, celery, scallion, and chile. Add the lime zest and juice, season generously, and stir to combine. Add the parsley and dill, stir, and set aside until needed.

5. Heat the tortillas on a lightly oiled ridged grill pan and keep warm in a clean dish towel.

6. Spread each tortilla with a light smear of sour cream, then top with some arugula leaves. followed by crispy potatoes, corn salsa, and some more sour cream. Finish with a squeeze of lime juice, dust with cinnamon, and serve.

ANGEL HAIR PASTA

with a lemon, dill & walnut sauce

SERVES 4

Pasta. Unsurprisingly, I have a major soft spot for the stuff—it's the carb that just keeps on giving and I am endlessly amazed at my ability to never tire of it. My mother often reminds me of my early obsession with ravioli, so this love affair clearly has deep roots. And while this gorgeously simple walnut sauce is probably not something my six-year-old self would have appreciated, this thirty-six year old version is borderline fanatical about it. Perhaps that's because it can made in mere minutes (we're talking ten, maximum) or maybe it's because a stripped-back pasta dish is all we need to fill that midweek comfort food hole. I affectionately refer to this recipe as "restoration in a bowl" and strongly recommend you earmark this page for I'm-in-a-rush-but-still-want-something-fabulous moments.

1 small garlic clove
grated zest and juice of 1 lemon
small bunch of dill, plus extra to garnish
1 teaspoon Dijon mustard
1 teaspoon capers
3 tablespoons extra virgin olive oil
¼ cup walnuts
10½ oz angel hair spaghetti
sea salt flakes and black pepper

1. Place the garlic, lemon zest and juice, dill, mustard, capers, and olive oil in a small blender or processor. Season generously and blend briefly to combine, then add the walnuts and blend again to form a coarse pestolike sauce.

2. Bring a large pan of salted water to a boil. Add the pasta and cook for 2 to 3 minutes, or just under the recommended cooking time. Drain the pasta, setting aside 7 tablespoons of the cooking water.

3. Return the pasta to the pan, season generously, and add the walnut sauce along with the reserved cooking water. Gently combine over low heat until all the strands are coated, then divide among bowls and serve garnished with a little extra dill.

ZA'ATAR ROASTED VEGETABLE PLATTER

with a carrot pesto & basil oil drizzle

SERVES 4

I have a thing about platters. I love having food arranged and displayed in such a way that makes it seem tactile and exciting. Roasted vegetables lend themselves particularly well to this method of serving, especially when paired with a chunky carrot pesto. Since I discovered carrot pesto a little while back, it's quickly overtaken all other varieties in my kitchen. Not only does it make for a great dressing but I also use it as a dip or sandwich spread and of course it's wonderful stirred through pasta too.

1 head of cauliflower, broken into large florets
1 head of broccoli, broken into large florets
2 large zucchini, cut diagonally into ½ inch pieces
1 tablespoon olive oil
grated zest of 1 lemon, plus juice of ½ lemon
1 heaping teaspoon za'atar
sea salt flakes and black pepper

Carrot pesto
2¼ cups coarsely chopped carrots
½ cup pine nuts
1 tablespoon cider vinegar
juice of ½ lemon
scant ¼ cup extra virgin olive oil
sea salt flakes and black pepper

Basil oil drizzle
large bunch of basil
¼ teaspoon sea salt flakes
¼ teaspoon black pepper
juice of ½ lemon
scant ¼ cup extra virgin olive oil

1. Preheat the oven to 425°F.
2. To make the carrot pesto, place the carrots in a food processor and pulse to break them into fine chunks. Add the pine nuts, vinegar, and lemon juice, season, and blitz for a few seconds before gradually pouring in the olive oil and continuing to bliz until the pesto is thick and creamy. Refrigerate until needed.
3. Arrange the vegetables on a baking sheet and pour over the olive oil and lemon juice. Add the za'atar and lemon zest and season generously. Toss to combine and roast for 35 to 40 minutes, turning the vegetables occasionally to ensure they roast evenly.
4. Transfer the roasted vegetables to a serving platter and generously adorn with the carrot pesto.
5. For the basil oil drizzle, place the basil leaves in a mortar and pestle with the salt and pepper and muddle until it forms a paste. Add the lemon juice and olive oil and vigorously combine. Season to taste, then drizzle over the roasted vegetables and serve.

SEASONED CAULIFLOWER

with a savory citrus sauce

SERVES 6

Cauliflower is my meat. This might seem like a strange thing to say but it really does fill that dreaded hole on the plate; not least because of its fibrous qualities but also because it soaks up any marinade especially well—all those nooks and crannies cry out for a suitably robust sauce and make it a terrific backdrop for most flavors. I often use this orange sauce with parsley and pistachios because it pairs beautifully with the cauliflower's delicate flavor. This dish makes a great simple appetizer, though it can also be served alongside an array of salads and sides for a more substantial meal that will be sure to wow.

1 head of cauliflower, outer leaves removed and cut into six equal-sized wedges

Marinade
1 tablespoon Dijon mustard
½ tablespoon maple syrup
½ tablespoon olive oil
grated zest and juice of ½ orange
¼ teaspoon sea salt flakes
pinch of white pepper

Savory citrus sauce
2 cups flat-leaf parsley
1 scallion
4 tablespoons toasted pistachios
grated zest and juice of ½ orange
1 green chile
2 tablespoons extra virgin olive oil
sea salt flakes and black pepper

To serve
scant ½ cup slivered pistachios
small handful of torn flat-leaf parsley
grated zest of ½ orange

1. Preheat the oven to 475°F.

2. Whisk the marinade ingredients together in a small bowl. Generously brush the cauliflower wedges with the marinade, setting aside a little for cooking.

3. Transfer the cauliflower wedges to a baking sheet and roast for 25 to 30 minutes, turning once and brushing with the reserved marinade, until browned.

4. Meanwhile, place all the sauce ingredients in a food processor and blend to combine (or pound the ingredients together using a mortar and pestle for a more rustic option).

5. To serve, dollop a generous spoonful of the sauce onto the center of 6 individual small serving plates and place a cauliflower wedge on top of each. Sprinkle over a few slivered pistachios, a little torn parsley, and some orange zest just before serving.

HOT LEMONY ARTICHOKE & SPINACH DIP

SERVES 4

I love a good dip and this one is a nice departure from the usual hummus on offer at parties. Its zesty notes are offset brilliantly by its unctuous creaminess, the result of a terrific cashew–tofu combo that sounds odd but totally works! Don't worry if you can only get your hands on antipasti-style jarred artichokes, simply rinse off any excess oil and herbs before using. Likewise, the nutritional yeast is not crucial; it adds a certain "cheesiness" that some people adore but it's not the deciding factor in the success of this simple but lovely little dish.

1⅓ cups cashews, soaked and drained (see page 8)

⅔ cup water

½ teaspoon sea salt flakes

½ teaspoon black pepper

grated zest and juice of 1 lemon

5¼ oz silken tofu

3 tablespoons nutritional yeast (optional)

½ tablespoon Dijon mustard

½ tablespoon olive oil

3 cups baby leaf spinach

5¼ oz precooked artichokes

1. Preheat the oven to 475°F.
2. Place the cashews in a blender with the measured water, salt, pepper, and half the lemon juice. Blend until smooth before adding the tofu, yeast (if using), and mustard. Season and blend on high speed for 5 to 7 minutes until completely smooth and pourable, scraping down the sides from time to time as you go.
3. Heat the olive oil in a pan over a low to medium heat, add the spinach, and cook for 1 to 2 minutes, or until gently wilted. Transfer to a blender together with the artichokes and lemon zest, season, and pulse to combine. Pour in 1 cup of the cashew and tofu cream and the remaining lemon juice, season generously, and pulse until the mixture just comes together but still retains some texture.
4. Transfer to a baking dish and bake for 20 minutes until browned, then remove from the oven and let cool for a few minutes before serving. It's great with crudités.

OAT & ORANGE BLOSSOM "SHROVE TUESDAY" PANCAKES

with chocolate sauce

MAKES 5

Almost crepe-thin, these oaty pancakes are a nod to the ones I used to enjoy on Shrove Tuesday with my family. The key to getting them as thin as possible is transferring the batter to a pitcher and practicing the "pour and swirl"—pouring the batter into the preheated pan and gently tipping the pan from side to side (in a sort of circular motion) until the batter meets the edges. And while these pancakes are wonderful served with a squeeze of lime and a drizzle of agave nectar, I've gone down the chocolate sauce route here for a bit of well-deserved indulgence. Pancake Day never tasted so good!

1½ cups rolled oats
½ teaspoon baking soda
pinch of sea salt flakes
scant 1 cup almond milk
juice of ½ orange
½ tablespoon orange blossom water
½ tablespoon agave nectar
7 tablespoons water, plus extra if necessary

1 to 2 tablespoons coconut oil
oat flakes, to decorate

Chocolate sauce
1 heaping tablespoon coconut oil
2 heaping tablespoons raw cacao powder or
  cocoa
1 tablespoon agave nectar
pinch of sea salt flakes

1. Place the oats in a small food processor or blender and blend to a fine flour. Transfer to a mixing bowl along with the baking soda and salt and stir to combine.

2. Whisk the almond milk, orange juice, orange blossom water, and agave nectar together in a separate bowl.

3. Make a well in the center of the flour and pour in the almond milk mixture together with the measured water and whisk to combine. The batter should be the consistency of light cream and tends to thicken over time, so thin it out with a little extra water as necessary. Transfer to a pitcher.

4. Heat 1 teaspoon of coconut oil in a nonstick skillet over medium to high heat. Pour in just enough batter to coat the bottom, swirling to ensure it reaches the edges. Cook for at least 5 minutes, or until bubbles form and the edges appeared cooked—the pancakes can be delicate, so be sure not to flip them too soon. Flip the pancake (or turn carefully with a wide spatula) then cook for another 3 to 5 minutes until thoroughly cooked. Transfer to a warmed plate and cover with a clean dish towel. Repeat until all the batter is used, adding an extra teaspoon of coconut oil to the pan between pancakes.

5. To make the chocolate sauce, heat the coconut oil in a saucepan until melted. Take it off the heat and whisk in the cacao, agave nectar, and salt until smooth and glossy. Pour into a small pitcher.

6. Fold the pancakes and arrange them on a large plate or platter. Pour over the chocolate sauce and sprinkle over a few oat flakes just before serving.

LEMON CHIA PUDDING

with a warm blackberry compote & toasted coconut

SERVES 2

Chia crops up regularly in my cooking. Those unassuming seeds that transform into tapioca-like pearls once they meet liquid have long held my fascination—not only because of their nutritional properties but also because they satisfy me until lunch. And while I try not to get too hung up on their "healthy" credentials, it's difficult to ignore the impressive benefits that range from their high fiber and protein content through to the essential omega-3 fatty acids they contain—though let's be honest, none of that truly matters if they're not up to scratch in the taste department. I like to bolster their neutral (some might say "nonexistent") flavor with a dash of citrus. The addition of lemon in this recipe really livens up breakfast time and also makes for an excellent brunch intro, especially when paired with this comforting warm blackberry compote. Like rice pudding and jam. Only better.

1 cup oat milk (*see* page 9),
    plus extra if necessary
3 tablespoons canned coconut cream
grated zest and juice of 1 small lemon or lime
pinch of pink Himalayan salt
3 tablespoons maple syrup
4 tablespoons chia seeds

Blackberry compote
generous 1 cup fresh blackberries
1 tablespoon maple syrup
juice of ½ orange

To serve
finely sliced orange peel
2 heaping tablespoons toasted coconut flakes

1. Whisk the oat milk, coconut cream, lemon zest and juice, salt, and syrup together in a bowl until combined. Stir through the chia seeds and refrigerate for at least an hour, preferably overnight.

2. To make the blackberry compote, bring the ingredients to a gentle simmer in a small saucepan and cook for 10 to 15 minutes until thick and syrupy. Lightly mash the berries, leaving a few whole, and set aside until needed.

3. Remove the pudding from the refrigerator and stir to loosen the mixture, adding a touch more oat milk if it is looking a little stiff.

4. Divide the pudding among shallow bowls, topping each with a large spoonful of the compote, some finely sliced orange peel, and a smattering of toasted coconut.

HOMEMADE CASHEW YOGURT

with griddled grapefruit

SERVES 2

Making your own yogurt can feel slightly overwhelming, particularly if you're unfamiliar with probiotics. Luckily this "cashew-gurt" is as straightforward as it gets, mainly because you have complete control over the texture and thickness without having to resort to tapioca starch or agar agar. I like my yogurt quite thick and unctuous, but if you prefer it thinner simply add more water. Delicately flavored with vanilla and lemon, this is a firm breakfast favorite.

1⅓ cups cashews
juice of ½ lemon
2 to 3 tablespoons maple syrup or other vegan
    sweetener
vanilla pod, seeds scraped
pinch of Himalayan salt
¾ to 1 cup water
3 probiotic capsules

Griddled grapefruit
½ tablespoon pomegranate molasses
2 tablespoons palm sugar
juice of ½ grapefruit
1 large grapefruit, peeled and cut into circles

1. To make the yogurt, place the cashews in a bowl, cover with water and let soak for 8 to 12 hours.
2. Drain and rinse the cashews, then place in a blender with the lemon juice, maple syrup, vanilla seeds, salt, and water (¾ cup for a thick yogurt and up to 1 cup for a lighter variety). Blend until completely smooth, scraping down the sides periodically.
3. Transfer the cashew mixture to a scrupulously clean bowl or jar and add the contents of the probiotic capsules. Whisk, cover with a clean tea towel or muslin cloth and set aside in a dark, dry place for up to 24 hours—or 48 hours for a more potent yogurt.
4. Once its fermented, refrigerate the yogurt until needed. It's best served chilled and will keep for up to a week.
5. To make the griddled grapefruit, whisk the pomegranate molasses, palm sugar, and grapefruit juice together until smooth. Heat a ridged grill pan over medium to high heat, add the grapefruit pieces, and cook until charred on both sides. Transfer the griddled grapefruit to the bowl and let marinate for 30 minutes. Arrange the grapefruit slices on a plate and serve with a spoonful of cashew yogurt.

CLEMENTINE & COCONUT LASSI

with a touch of pink Himalayan salt

SERVES 2

My biggest regret about visiting India almost a decade ago was not consuming more lassi while I was there. Not yet vegan at the time, this was my first proper foray into vegetarian food and it really opened my eyes. Traditional lassi contains dairy, of course, but I think coconut yogurt is an even better way of enjoying this satisfyingly exotic little drink. The addition of salt is crucial and sets this lassi apart from a regular smoothie—balancing the sweet and slightly sour flavors. I prefer to drink it chilled and poured into glasses filled with ice—a creamy, moreish concoction to be sipped and savored.

⅔ cup coconut yogurt
juice of 2 clementines
½ ripe mango
1¼ cups chilled coconut water
1 tablespoon agave nectar
pinch of pink Himalayan salt

To serve
pink Himalayan salt
ground coriander
torn basil leaves

1. Place all the ingredients into a high-speed blender and blend until completely combined.
2. Divide between glasses, sprinkle over a touch of salt and a dusting of ground coriander along with some torn fresh basil. Enjoy immediately or chill in the refrigerator for up to a day until needed.

FRESH

SMOOTHIE 101

Smoothies have fast become a regular morning feature in my life. Aside from being incredibly delicious and quick to make, they are also a great way to inject some additional servings of fruit and vegetables into your day. Because I rarely have the same fruit in my bowl or veggies in my refrigerator from week to week I've developed a little strategy for getting the most out of (and into) my smoothies with whatever I happen to have in my kitchen. If you're anything like me you're bound to have a least one item from each list to hand, making it supereasy to create the most balanced smoothie bowl.

LIQUID	GREENS	FRUIT	OTHER
plant milk (soy, oat, almond, coconut, or other)	kale	banana (frozen or fresh)	nut butter (such as peanut, almond, cashew, or hazelnut)
juice (such as orange, grapefruit, apple, lemon, or lime)	spinach	apple	dairy-free yogurt (such as soy, coconut, or almond)
coconut water	Tuscan kale	pear	avocado
filtered water	romaine lettuce	pineapple	soaked nuts (cashews, almonds etc.)
	broccoli stalks	melon	rolled oats
	parsley	mango	seeds (such as chia, hemp, or flaxseed)
	mint	nectarine or peach	fresh ginger root or turmeric
	celery	berries (frozen or fresh)	spices and powders (such as cinnamon, cacao, maca, spirulina, chlorella, or acai)
	peas		

1. Place your chosen liquid in the bottom of a blender, add the remaining ingredients, and blend until completely smooth.
2. Transfer to a bowl, add your choice of toppings, and serve.

Here are three combinations I currently have on rotation—simply follow the method on the opposite page. Strangely enough, none of these smoothies contain banana.

NECTARINE & OATS

Top with raspberries, sliced nectarine, and poppy seeds. Make this ahead of time and let it chill overnight for a super-quick, nutritious breakfast.

2 ripe nectarines or peaches
scant ½ cup raspberries
2 medjool dates, pitted
½ cup rolled oats
¼ cup slivered almonds or 1 heaping teaspoon almond butter

¼ teaspoon vanilla powder (or seeds from ½ vanilla bean)
7 tablespoons oat or almond milk
3 heaping tablespoons coconut or soy yogurt
juice of ½ lemon

ULTIMATE "NO BANANA" BERRY BOWL

Serve this parfait-style with homemade rawnola (*see* page 46) and a handful of frozen berries. For it to taste at its best, this must be eaten immediately.

1 cup frozen mixed berries
1 celery stalk
scant ¼ cup rice milk
scant ¼ cup orange juice

3 heaping tablespoons soy or other dairy-free yogurt
1 heaping tablespoon cashew butter
2 heaping tablespoons milled flaxseed
1 tablespoon maple syrup

SUPER GREEN SMOOTHIE

For a glorious, pulp-free green juice add slightly more water at the blending stage and strain it through a nut-milk bag or cheesecloth before serving. This smoothie refrigerates well.

scant 1 cup filtered or coconut water
5¼ oz fresh pineapple
1 apple
1 thumb-sized piece of fresh ginger root, peeled

1¾ oz spinach
1¾ oz kale
juice of ½ grapefruit

DATE & COCONUT RAWNOLA

MAKES 6 SERVINGS

My love for granola really knows no bounds and I'm always looking for new and interesting ways to tweak how I make it. It didn't occur to me until relatively recently that the raw mixture itself—almost like cookie dough—is really rather wonderful, so why bake it at all? The crucial point here is texture, so go easy on the blending; once the mixture reaches the "sticky rubble" stage it's time to stop or else you begin to enter bliss-ball territory (not necessarily a bad thing, but not what we're after here). I like to set aside half the coconut for a quick pulse toward the end so you're left with lots of lovely flakes but feel free to add it all at once or play around by varying the nuts and dried fruit—I'm thinking an apricot and pistachio combo would be spectacular.

1 cup rolled oats	**⅓ cup raisins**
scant ½ cup almonds	**1 teaspoon ground cinnamon**
½ cup coconut flakes	**¼ teaspoon sea salt flakes**
4 medjool dates, pitted	

1. Place the oats, almonds, and half the coconut flakes in a food processor and pulse briefly to break down.

2. Add the dates, raisins, cinnamon, and salt and blitz for 1 to 2 minutes to form a sticky rubble—the mix will appear dry initially but will eventually form sticky clusters (be careful not to overwork it). Add the remaining coconut flakes and pulse to combine.

3. Transfer the rawnola to a clean jar and store in a cool place or the refrigerator—it will keep for up to 10 days.

4. Serve with your favorite dairy-free yogurt, with plant milk and fresh fruit, or on its own as a snack.

CARROT, CUCUMBER & APPLE SALAD

with a ginger & passion fruit dressing

SERVES 2 TO 4

Sometimes I like to return to familiar ingredients in a bid to find new and exciting ways to make them shine. I always have an apple, carrots, and cucumber to hand, which makes this simple salad a bit of a go-to recipe of mine. I've resisted the temptation to add a smattering of seeds here (although sunflower and pumpkin seeds would work particularly well), instead letting the glorious ginger dressing take center stage—it really is that good! For something so simple, this salad has the ability to be a real talking point when arranged on a platter and garnished with what is perhaps my favorite mix of herbs. As the Barefoot Contessa would say, it's carrot salad "with the volume turned up" … right up.

1 large carrot, peeled and cut into thin sticks
½ cucumber, halved lengthwise, seeds removed, and cut into half-moons
1 celery stalk, finely chopped
1 heaping tablespoon coarsely chopped dill
1 heaping tablespoon coarsely chopped cilantro
1 heaping tablespoon coarsely chopped mint
1 large apple, peeled, cored, and sliced

Ginger & passion fruit dressing
1 thumb-sized piece of fresh ginger root, peeled and finely grated
1 heaping teaspoon Dijon mustard
juice of ½ lemon
½ tablespoon cider vinegar
½ tablespoon agave nectar
1 passion fruit, seeds strained
3 tablespoons extra virgin olive oil
sea salt flakes and black pepper

1. Put the carrot, cucumber, and celery pieces in a large bowl.
2. To make the dressing, add all the ingredients to a separate bowl, season generously, and whisk together vigorously until emulsified.
3. Pour two-thirds of the dressing over the salad and, using your hands, toss gently to combine.
4. Add the chopped herbs to the bowl, setting aside a small handful for garnish. Gently toss to ensure they are evenly dispersed, then pile the salad onto a large platter or plate and arrange the apple slices in and around it.
5. Pour over the remaining dressing and sprinkle over the rest of the herbs to finish.

SALSA-STYLE PANZANELLA SALAD

with griddled nectarines

SERVES 2 TO 4

This dish epitomizes summer for me. A gorgeously vibrant salsa interspersed with crisp griddled tortilla chips and sweet charred nectarines, it is a stunning sharing plate—perfect for a relaxed girls' night in. For me, the ideal salsa lies in the "chop"; I am fastidious about keeping each individual ingredient perfectly proportioned, guaranteeing the ultimate bite each and every time. I like to use the crisp edge of the tortilla to cut through the soft nectarine before scooping up the salsa, ensuring maximum eating pleasure.

2 large flour tortillas
scant ¼ cup olive oil
2 ripe nectarines, halved, pitted, and cut into
 thick slices
3 tomatoes, diced
1 large ripe avocado, diced
1 small green chile, minced
1 shallot, minced
juice of ½ lime

small bunch of leaf parsley, coarsely chopped
sea salt flakes and black pepper

Dressing
1 ripe nectarine, pitted
juice of 1 lime
1 heaping teaspoon palm sugar
1 heaping teaspoon pomegranate molasses
sea salt flakes and black pepper

1. Heat a ridged grill pan over medium to high heat. Lightly brush the tortillas with the olive oil and cut into large triangles. Griddle the tortillas for 3 to 4 minutes on each side until crispy and charred, then remove from the pan.

2. Add the nectarine slices to the ridged grill pan and cook for 1 to 2 minutes on each side until lightly charred.

3. Put the tomatoes, avocado, chile, and shallot in a mixing bowl, squeeze over the lime juice, and season generously with salt and pepper. Stir through the parsley, setting aside a little for garnish.

4. To make the dressing, place all the ingredients in a blender, season, and blend together to form a smooth puree.

5. Pile the salsa into the center of a shallow bowl or dish and arrange the tortillas and griddled nectarine around it. Drizzle over the dressing, garnish with the remaining parsley, and serve.

CAULI-RICE MAKI ROLLS

with beet & apple

SERVES 2 TO 4

I am often put off making sushi mainly because I can rarely be bothered to boil, cool, and season the rice but since swapping to cauli-rice it's become much more of a regular feature on my menu. The fillings vary, although recently I've been quite taken with this beet and apple pairing—having that sweet crunch in there truly makes all the difference. Cauli-rice in itself isn't terribly exciting but adding a little lemon zest, chile, and herbs like this suddenly transforms it into something quite special.

4 to 8 nori seaweed sheets

small handful of watercress or
    pea shoots

2 small cooked beet, cut lengthwise into
    thin strips

½ cucumber, cut into thin sticks

1 apple, peeled, cored, and cut into thin sticks

Cauli-rice

1 small head of cauliflower, broken into
    florets

½ green chile

1 thumb-sized piece of fresh ginger root,
    peeled

small handful of leaf parsley

small handful of fresh mint

grated zest of 1 lemon

sea salt flakes and black pepper

Dipping sauce

3 heaping tablespoons egg-free mayo

1 heaping tablespoon Thai sweet chili sauce

juice of ½ lemon

1. To make the cauli-rice, add the cauliflower florets to a food processor with the rest of the ingredients, season generously, and pulse together to form a nubbly, coarse "rice."

2. For the dipping sauce, put the ingredients in a small bowl and mix together well. Set aside.

3. Lay a nori sheet on a sushi rolling mat, shiny-side down, and cover three-quarters of the sheet with the cauli-rice, leaving a gap at the end farthest away from you.

4. Beginning with the watercress and following with the beet, cucumber, and then the apple, layer the ingredients in a horizontal line across the middle of the sheet. Begin to roll the nori sheet up away from you, tucking it tightly as you go and dabbing the gap at the end with a little water to seal. Repeat with the remaining nori sheets and filling ingredients.

5. Fill a large pitcher with water and use it to wet a sharp knife. Shake any excess water off the knife before slicing the sushi rolls into equal-sized circles. Transfer them to a platter and serve with the dipping sauce.

ROMAINE LETTUCE WRAPS

with spicy coconut chickpeas & zesty cauli-rice

SERVES 2

Goodness, these are good. I know that lettuce wraps reek of dullness but these are too tasty to be ignored. I recommend getting the biggest, most badass romaine you can find—lackluster leaves really won't do here. It's also crucial to let the chickpeas cool slightly before assembling the wraps, otherwise you might have end up with a droop situation on your hands.

1 head of romaine lettuce, leaves separated

Zesty cauli-rice
1 small head of cauliflower, broken into florets
large bunch of cilantro
2 scallions
grated zest and juice of ½ large lemon
1 heaping teaspoon ground cumin
½ teaspoon sea salt flakes
generous ⅓ cup toasted slivered almonds
scant ¼ cup raisins or chopped apricots
black pepper

Spicy coconut chickpeas
1 heaping teaspoon coconut oil
2 shallots, finely sliced

1¾ cups canned chickpeas, rinsed and drained
1 teaspoon smoked paprika
1 heaping teaspoon tomato paste
8 cherry tomatoes, halved
½ cup canned coconut milk
1 teaspoon sambal oelek (or other chili paste)
1 heaping tablespoon finely chopped cilantro, plus extra to serve
sea salt flakes and black pepper

Avocado & dill crema
1 ripe avocado
juice of ½ lemon
scant 3 tablespoons canned coconut milk
small handful of dill, finely chopped
sea salt flakes and black pepper

1. To make the cauli-rice, add the cauliflower florets to a food processor with the cilantro, scallions, lemon zest, cumin, and salt. Pulse together to form a nubbly, coarse "rice," then transfer to a large bowl. Add the slivered almonds, raisins, and lemon juice and stir to combine. Check for seasoning, stir, and set aside until needed.

2. For the spicy coconut chickpeas, heat the coconut oil in a small skillet over medium heat, add the shallots, and sauté for 3 to 4 minutes until translucent. Add the chickpeas and smoked paprika, lightly season with salt and pepper, and sauté for 1 to 2 minutes, then stir in the tomato paste and cherry tomatoes. Pour over the coconut milk and a splash of water, bring to a simmer, and cook, covered with a lid, for 10 minutes, or until the tomatoes have begun to soften.

3. Stir through the sambal oelek and continue to simmer for 3 to 4 minutes until the sauce has thickened and reduced. Stir through the cilantro, then remove from the heat and let cool for 5 minutes (you want to serve this warm not piping hot).

4. Meanwhile, make the crema by mashing the avocado in a bowl with a fork until smooth. Add the lemon juice, coconut milk, and dill, season generously, and mix together until thick and creamy.

5. To assemble the wraps, spread the lettuce leaves first with the crema, then layer over a generous amount of cauli-rice and top with a spoonful of the warm chickpeas. Sprinkle over a final smattering of cilantro to finish.

BACK-TO-FRONT BIBIMBAP BOWL

SERVES 2

I've flipped the typical bibimbap on its head here, using a cold (raw) broccoli rice base and keeping the hot element for the toppings. Many such bowls typically contain some egg component so I've included my ultimate tofu scramble here, which is my plant-based attempt to replicate that same eggy texture—it's surprisingly convincing. To make this four-part bowl a touch more straightforward and help minimize the kitchen mess, I use the same pan for each element, wiping it clean each time in between. In true bibimbap style, of course, don't forget to give it all a good mix before digging in!

Broccoli rice
1 small head of broccoli, broken into florets and stalk set aside
small bunch of flat-leaf parsley
grated zest of 1 lemon
sea salt flakes and black pepper

Spinach
1 teaspoon coconut oil
10½ oz spinach
1 tablespoon tamari or soy sauce
1 tablespoon rice mirin
squeeze of lemon juice
1 tablespoon sesame seeds

Carrot
1 garlic clove
1 thumb-sized piece of fresh ginger root, peeled
2 tablespoons toasted sesame oil
1 tablespoon tamari
1 teaspoon cider vinegar

juice of ½ lemon
1 teaspoon palm sugar
1 teaspoon coconut oil
2 large carrots, cut into ribbons

Scrambled tofu
1 teaspoon coconut oil
1 small onion, halved lengthwise and sliced into half-moons
10½ oz firm tofu, crumbled
1 heaping teaspoon ground turmeric
2 tablespoons tamari
1 teaspoon dried red pepper flakes
juice of ½ lemon
scant ¼ cup soy milk (or other plant milk, see page 9)
1 large tomato, diced

To serve
freshly chopped flat-leaf parsley
Sriracha or other chili sauce
cucumber slices

1. To make the broccoli rice, add the broccoli florets and stalk to a food processor together with the parsley and lemon zest. Season generously and pulse together to form a nubbly, coarse "rice." Set aside until needed.

2. For the spinach, melt the coconut oil in a skillet over medium heat, add the spinach, tamari, rice mirin, and lemon juice and cook until wilted. Add the sesame seeds, toss to combine, and transfer to a warm oven.

3. For the carrot, whisk all the ingredients, except the coconut oil and carrot ribbons, together in an ovenproof bowl to form a dressing. Wipe the pan clean with paper towels, then add the coconut oil and

carrot ribbons and cook over medium heat for 3 to 4 minutes until tender. Add the carrot to the bowl with the dressing and toss to combine, then transfer to the oven to keep warm.

4. To make the scrambled tofu, wipe the pan clean with paper towels again, then add the coconut oil and onion, season, and cook for 3 to 4 minutes over medium heat until the onion begins to soften. Stir in the tofu and turmeric and season generously, then add the tamari, red pepper flakes, lemon juice, and soy milk and cook for 10 minutes, or until the tofu is cooked through. Add the tomato, season again, and sauté for another 5 minutes. Remove from the heat.

5. To serve, divide the broccoli rice among two bowls and top with the wilted spinach, dressed carrot ribbons, and scrambled tofu. Garnish with freshly chopped parsley, lashings of hot sauce (I recommend Sriracha), and freshly sliced cucumber.

GLASS NOODLE SALAD

SERVES 2 TO 4

Rice noodles are a godsend. If ever I'm pushed for time or haven't the energy to cook properly, these are what I wheel out—I call it a "shortcut with style." While these are perfectly wonderful eaten alone, I also often serve them as part of a larger meal or buffet so people can wrangle with the noodles themselves and enjoy their clean-tasting, Asian-inspired vibe. They also happen to look rather pretty, especially adorned with a sprinkling of black sesame seeds to set off the glorious, pale green hue. Grab your chopsticks and let's go.

2 rice noodle nests
generous ¾ cup frozen shelled edamame
½ cucumber, cut into ribbons
3½ oz sugar snap peas, sliced diagonally

Zesty Asian dressing
1 small red chile, finely chopped
1 thumb-sized piece of fresh ginger root,
    peeled and grated

grated zest and juice of 1 lime
2 tablespoons tamari
½ tablespoon sesame oil
1½ tablespoons maple syrup
½ tablespoon rice mirin

To serve
2 scallions, sliced
2 tablespoons black sesame seeds

1. Place the rice noodles and edamame in a large bowl and cover with freshly boiled water. Let soak for 8 to 10 minutes, stirring occasionally with chopsticks to break up the nests of noodles. When the noodles are soft, drain and set aside.

2. To make the dressing, mix the chile and ginger together in a small bowl to form a paste, then add the remaining ingredients and whisk together vigorously.

3. Pour the dressing over the noodles and combine, using your hands. Add the cucumber and sugar snap peas to the bowl and mix to combine. Refrigerate until needed.

4. When ready to serve, garnish with the scallion and sesame seeds.

WATERMELON, WATERCRESS & CUCUMBER SALAD

SERVES 4

Nothing says summer like a watermelon salad. Tossed with ribbons of fresh cucumber and doused in a creamy tahini sauce, this is one seriously beautiful bowl that is almost (almost) too beautiful to eat. This salad might be simple but it packs a punch—full of fresh flavors and contrasting textures, it never fails to impress.

2¾ oz watercress
1 small watermelon (about 1¾ lb), rind removed and cut into thick triangular wedges
1 small cucumber, cut into ribbons
1 celery stalk, finely sliced

1 scallion, finely sliced
1 heaping tablespoon chopped mint
scant ¼ cup pumpkin seeds
1 x "Goes-with-Everything" Tahini Sauce (*see* page 151)

1. Cover a large plate or serving platter with the watercress, then layer over the watermelon wedges and top with the cucumber, celery, and scallion.

2. To make the tahini dressing, put all the ingredients in a bowl and whisk to combine. Taste and adjust the seasoning.

3. Drizzle a few tablespoons of the tahini sauce over the salad and finish by scattering over the mint and pumpkin seeds.

HAWAIIAN MANGO POKE BOATS

SERVES 4

Endive can be a "love it or loathe it" type of leaf. While my husband generally struggles with its inherent bitterness, he adores these little poke boats—smoky, sweet, and fresh, their intriguing flavor combination often becomes a talking point … for all the right reasons, I might add. The mango's soft flesh absorbs the marinade beautifully while still retaining its all-important form. Having never been to Hawaii myself (it's on the bucket list!), I can't confirm if these resemble the real thing but they do emphatically work—and in the grand scheme of things that's really all that matters.

2 tablespoons tamari

1 tablespoon cold-pressed sesame oil

1 tablespoon maple syrup

juice of ½ orange

1 tablespoon lemon or lime juice

1 large ripe mango, peeled, pit removed, and cut into bite-sized pieces

2 scallions, finely chopped

small handful of cilantro leaves, coarsely chopped

1 tablespoon black sesame seeds

1 head of endive, leaves separated

1. In a bowl, whisk the tamari, sesame oil, maple syrup, orange and lemon juices together vigorously until combined.

2. Add the mango to the bowl and stir to combine, then cover with plastic wrap and refrigerate for 1 hour. Remove the mango using a slotted spoon and transfer to a shallow bowl.

3. Add the scallion, cilantro, and black sesame seeds to the mango bowl, setting aside a little of each for garnish.

4. Arrange the endive leaves on a large plate or platter. Fill each leaf "boat" with a spoonful of the mango poke, garnish with the remaining scallion, cilantro, and sesame seeds and serve.

CORN FRITTERS

with quick-pickled carrot

MAKES 8 TO 10 FRITTERS

I'm sure many of you already have a go-to fritter recipe up your sleeve but I still think these are worth your consideration. I try to limit how often I make them because I end up consuming most of them on my own. I also make slightly small versions for parties (they're great finger food) as well as serving them at brunch like this topped with a super-fresh "quick pickle" and accompanied by tumblers of green juice. I can't think of a better way to kick-start the weekend, can you?

¾ cup canned corn kernels	Quick-pickled carrot
scant ⅔ cup gram (chickpea) flour	1 large carrot, cut into fine ribbons
¼ teaspoon baking powder	juice of ½ lemon
½ teaspoon sea salt flakes	juice of ½ orange
¼ teaspoon black pepper	1 tablespoon cider vinegar
juice of 1 lemon	1 tablespoon palm sugar or maple syrup
5 tablespoons soy milk	2 teaspoons sea salt flakes
1 corn cob, kernels removed	scant ¼ cup golden raisins
3 scallions, chopped	1 heaping tablespoon finely chopped
2 to 3 tablespoons canola oil	cilantro leaves

1. For the quick-pickled carrot, add the carrot to a shallow bowl together with the lemon and orange juices, cider vinegar, palm sugar, and salt. Stir through the golden raisins and let soak for 1 to 2 minutes, then mix together with your hands to combine and refrigerate until needed.

2. Add the canned corn kernels to a blender and blitz to a smooth puree.

3. Whisk the flour, baking powder, salt, and pepper together in a large bowl. Add the corn puree, lemon juice, and soy milk and stir together to form a thick batter.

4. Stir the raw corn kernels and scallion through the batter and season generously.

5. Heat the canola oil in a large skillet over medium to high heat, add tablespoonfuls of the batter to the pan, and cook the fritters in batches of two or three for 5 minutes on each side until crispy and golden. Transfer the fritters to a plate lined with paper towels to soak up any excess oil.

6. Repeat using all the remaining batter, being sure not to overcrowd the pan as you go.

7. Remove the pickled carrot from the refrigerator and stir through the chopped cilantro. Serve alongside the corn fritters.

MELON, AVOCADO & LIMA BEAN SALAD

with a jalapeño & lime dressing

SERVES 2 TO 4

This melon and lima bean salad is a recent favorite of mine. Because it works equally well as a side dish as it does as a complete meal, I find myself making it more and more often. The colors are a feast for the eyes and a peculiarly soothing trio—there's something about the soft orange and beige and smattering of pale green that exudes calm.

½ ripe cantaloupe melon, seeds and rind removed, and cut lengthwise into thick slices
1 large ripe avocado
scant 1 cup canned lima beans, rinsed and drained
small handful of mint, chopped
1 scallion, finely sliced

Jalapeño & lime dressing
1 heaping tablespoon minced red jalapeños
1 echalion or banana shallot, finely chopped
juice of 1 small lime
3 tablespoons extra virgin olive oil
½ tablespoon agave nectar, plus extra if necessary
¼ teaspoon sea salt flakes

1. Place the melon and avocado slices on a plate or platter and fan them out to separate them slightly.

2. Place the dressing ingredients in a bowl and whisk vigorously to combine. Season with salt to taste, adding a little more agave nectar for extra sweetness if needed.

3. Put the beans in a shallow dish, pour over half the dressing, and toss to combine. Stir through 1 tablespoon of the chopped mint, then spoon the lima beans over the melon and avocado. Drizzle over the remaining dressing and sprinkle over the scallion and remaining mint before serving.

POLENTA PIZZA

with spinach & roasted squash

SERVES 4 TO 6

Polenta is a bit of an obsession of my mine. I enjoy it for breakfast, adore it cut into wedges and fried, and think it makes a pretty epic substitute for mashed potatoes. But this easy pizza crust might just pip everything else to the post when it comes to how best to consume this super-versatile ingredient. Basically a fancy vehicle for toppings, this crispy, crunchy, flavorful base brings an unexpected wow factor to the table. Perfect for parties, it's sure to make even the most low-key affair go off with a bang.

Base
3 cups water
generous 1 cup cornmeal
1 tablespoon extra virgin olive oil
sea salt flakes and black pepper

Pizza sauce
3 tablespoons strained tomatoes
1 heaping tablespoon tomato paste
1 teaspoon oregano
1 garlic clove, minced
½ tablespoon maple syrup
½ tablespoon balsamic vinegar
scant ¼ cup water
sea salt flakes and black pepper

Toppings
**½ butternut squash, peeled and cut into
    bite-sized pieces**
1 heaping teaspoon oregano

1 tablespoon olive oil
7 oz spinach
2 shallots, sliced
**2 heaping tablespoons freshly chopped basil,
    plus extra to garnish**
2 tablespoons pumpkin seeds
**2 tablespoons nutritional yeast (optional),
    plus extra to garnish**
sea salt flakes and black pepper

"Cheesy" sunflower seed sauce
½ cup sunflower seeds
1 small garlic clove, minced
juice of ½ orange
1 teaspoon Dijon mustard
1 teaspoon maple syrup
½ teaspoon sea salt flakes
1 tablespoon nutritional yeast (optional)
½ cup water

1. Preheat the oven to 425°F. Line a baking sheet with parchment paper.
2. For the base, place the measured water in a saucepan and bring to a boil. Generously salt the water, whisk in the cornmeal, and cook over medium heat, stirring vigorously, for 15 to 20 minutes, or until it thickens. Add the oil, season well, and continue to cook, stirring, until it becomes rubbery and pliable.
3. Tip the cornmeal mixture onto the prepared baking sheet and spread it to the edges using a spatula. Transfer to the refrigerator and leave for 30 minutes to firm.
4. Meanwhile, prepare the toppings. Put the squash, oregano, and olive oil in a bowl and toss to coat. Season generously and roast for 30 minutes, or until golden and crispy. Remove from the oven and set aside until needed.

5. Increase the heat to 475°F and bring a large saucepan of water to a boil. Add the spinach to the pan and cook until wilted, then remove with a slotted spoon and squeeze out any excess liquid before grinding to a coarse pulp. Season and set aside until needed.

6. To make the pizza sauce, add the strained tomatoes, tomato paste, oregano, garlic, maple syrup, balsamic vinegar, and measured water to a bowl and whisk together to combine. Season and set aside.

7. Once firm, bake the pizza base for 20 to 25 minutes until the edges begin to crisp.

8. Spread the base with the pizza sauce and top with the sliced shallots, wilted spinach, basil, roasted squash, pumpkin seeds, and the nutritional yeast, if using. Bake for another 15 to 20 minutes, or until the edges are crispy and golden.

9. Meanwhile, place all the "cheesy" sauce ingredients in a bowl and blend together with a handheld blender until completely smooth.

10. To serve, cut the pizza into squares, drizzle over the sauce, and garnish with a little extra basil and/or nutritional yeast.

"MADE IN MINUTES" MINTED PEA MASH

SERVES 2 TO 4

As much as I adore potatoes, sometimes I really do fancy a change. And while peas might not be at the top of most people's lists when asked to name their favorite veg, I think they are something of an underappreciated gem. This puree is the perfect accompaniment to any evening meal, whether it's a pie, roasted celeriac steaks, or even marinated tofu. Wonderfully versatile, it can be made and on the table in mere minutes.

1 tablespoon olive oil
1 leek, trimmed and sliced
½ vegetable bouillon cube
1 large garlic clove, unpeeled
1½ cups water

scant 2¼ cups frozen peas
1 heaping tablespoon canned coconut cream
1 heaping tablespoon finely chopped mint
sea salt flakes and black pepper

1. Heat the olive oil in a small saucepan over medium heat. Add the leek, season, and sweat for 2 to 3 minutes until softened.

2. Add the bouillon cube and garlic clove to the pan, cover with the water, and bring to a boil, then add the peas, reduce the heat to a simmer, and cook gently for 2 to 3 minutes until the peas are just cooked through.

3. Drain the peas and transfer to a food processor. Unpeel the garlic clove and add it to the processor together with the coconut cream, then season and pulse until the mixture forms a coarse puree.

4. Return the pea mixture to the pan, stir through the mint, and gently heat through before serving.

WARM POTATO & SAMPHIRE SALAD

SERVES 4

When it's in season, I buy samphire by the bucket-load and because it makes a limited appearance I desperately try to make the most of it. Often I'll stir it through freshly cooked pasta before finishing the dish with a squeeze of lemon juice (bliss!), but I'm also partial to it in a warm potato salad. I boil the potatoes first and then let them crisp in the skillet, which not only saves time but also gives them an almost roast-tatty texture. With the naturally salty samphire, it's a match made in heaven.

1 lb 2 oz ruby gem potatoes (or other salad potatoes)	juice of ½ lemon
	2 scallions, sliced
1 tablespoon canola oil	2 tablespoons finely chopped dill
3¼ oz samphire	sea salt flakes and black pepper

1. Add the potatoes to a saucepan of generously salted water, cover with a lid, and bring to a boil, then reduce the heat to a gentle simmer and cook for 15 to 20 minutes, or until tender. Drain and let cool for 2 to 3 minutes before halving.

2. Heat the oil in a large skillet over high heat. Add the samphire and stir-fry over high heat until tender. Season with pepper and squeeze over a little lemon juice, then remove from the pan and set aside.

3. Add the potatoes to the pan cut-side down and fry for 5 to 10 minutes until crisp, shaking the pan very occasionally but trying not to move them too much as they cook. Season generously.

4. Return the samphire to the pan along with the scallions. Cook for 2 minutes, then remove from the heat, squeeze over the rest of the lemon juice, stir through the dill, and serve.

RAW CURRIED ZUCCHINI NOODLES

SERVES 2 TO 4

I don't go in for a tremendous amount of spiralizing but when I do it's usually to make this dish. It could be considered something of a "raw ramen bowl" due to (a) its convenience and (b) its comfort-food credentials—not a duo to be sniffed at. Best eaten fresh, these curried noodles frequently appear on my summer lunchtime menu and, despite the inclusion of mango and dates, the sauce used to coat them manages to remain surprisingly savory. Even if you have your reservations about raw food, I urge you to give this recipe a go.

2 large zucchini, trimmed
1 ripe mango, peeled, pit removed, and sliced
scant ½ cup soaked cashews
1 yellow bell pepper, cored and seeded
2 medjool dates, pitted
2 heaping teaspoons mild curry powder

juice of ½ lime
small bunch of cilantro leaves, finely
    chopped, plus extra to garnish
sea salt flakes and black pepper

1.   Using a spiralizer, cut the zucchini into long, thin noodles (or alternatively, slice them into thin ribbons using a vegetable peeler). Transfer the noodles to a large bowl.

2.   Add the mango, cashews, yellow bell pepper, dates, curry powder, and lime juice to a blender or food processor, season generously, and blitz to form a smooth sauce.

3.   Pour the sauce over the zucchini and sprinkle over the cilantro. Toss gently until the noodles are completely coated, then divide among bowls and garnish with a little extra chopped cilantro. Serve.

SPICE IT UP!

MINI BLACK-BEAN CHIMICHANGAS

with an avocado dip

SERVES 2 TO 3

Black beans and avocado are a timeless pairing, and one I have a particular fondness for. While I've occasionally tampered with the filling and the dip concoction here, nothing comes remotely close to the addictiveness of this combination (garlicky white beans and pesto has been the closest contender). I tend to think the old adage "if it ain't broke …" is particularly applicable here: not exactly groundbreaking chimichanga territory, but when it tastes this good, who cares?

5 tablespoons olive oil
6 taco-sized tortillas

Refried black beans
1 tablespoon olive oil
1 onion, finely chopped
1 garlic clove, minced
1¾ cups canned black beans, with their liquid
1 bay leaf
1 tablespoon minced pickled jalapeños
sea salt flakes and black pepper

Avocado dip
½ ripe avocado
1 tablespoon plain coconut or soy yogurt
1 tablespoon tahini
juice of ½ lime
1 garlic clove, minced
sea salt flakes and black pepper

1. For the refried beans, heat the olive oil in a saucepan over medium heat. Add the onion, season, and sweat for 2 to 3 minutes, or until translucent.

2. Add the garlic to the pan and sauté until aromatic, then add the black beans and their liquid together with the bay leaf and jalapeños. Season generously and simmer for 20 minutes until the mixture is relatively thick and the beans have softened further, then remove from the heat and coarsely mash, leaving a few beans whole for texture. Set aside until needed.

3. To make the avocado dip, place the avocado, yogurt, tahini, lime juice, and garlic in a blender. Season, add a splash of water, and blend until completely smooth. Refrigerate until needed.

4. Heat the olive oil in a small skillet over medium to high heat. Add a small piece of tortilla to check the temperature—if it is crispy and golden after 30 seconds then the oil is at the right temperature for frying.

5. Place a tortilla on a counter, add a spoonful of the black bean mixture to the lower half, and tuck in both sides before folding over the nearest edge. Carefully but firmly roll the tortilla up into a log and dampen the edges with a little water to secure. Repeat with the remaining tortillas and filling.

6. Carefully lower the chimichangas into the hot oil in batches and fry for 2 to 3 minutes on each side until crispy and golden (being careful not to overcrowd the pan). Remove from the pan and drain on a plate lined with paper towels, then serve immediately alongside the avocado dip.

SPICE IT UP!

STIR-FRIED SOBA NOODLES

with griddled eggplant medallions

SERVES 2 TO 4

I might have a ridged grill pan problem. Whether fruit or veg, it will soon feel the piercingly hot ridges of my well-used turquoise grill pan. Eggplants lend themselves especially well to a good charring. The miso sauce is rich and satisfying and, well, the soba noodles are a bit of a no-brainer. This is fuss-free food with a touch of panache—and all it requires is a bit of grill-pan bravery. Go forth and sear!

1 large garlic clove, minced

1 thumb-sized piece of fresh ginger root, peeled and minced

1 green chile, minced

1½ teaspoons Sriracha or other chili sauce

3 tablespoons tamari or soy sauce

1 tablespoon sesame oil

juice of ½ orange

1 tablespoon lime juice (or lemon juice)

½ tablespoon maple syrup

7 oz soba noodles

1 tablespoon coconut oil

1 small onion, finely sliced

3½ oz Brussels sprouts, finely sliced

5¼ oz Tuscan kale, finely sliced

1 heaping tablespoon coarsely chopped cilantro leaves

1 heaping teaspoon dried red pepper flakes

sea salt flakes and black pepper

Eggplant medallions

2 tablespoons miso paste

1 tablespoon tamari or soy sauce

1 tablespoon rice mirin

1 tablespoon toasted sesame oil

juice of ½ orange

½ tablespoon maple syrup

1 large eggplant, cut into ½ inch circles

1. For the eggplant medallions, place the miso, tamari, mirin, sesame oil, orange juice, and maple syrup in a bowl and whisk vigorously to combine. Add the eggplant circles and toss to coat evenly, then let marinate for 10 minutes.

2. Add the garlic, ginger, chile, Sriracha, tamari, sesame oil, orange juice, lime juice, and maple syrup to a bowl and whisk to combine. Set aside.

3. Put a ridged grill pan over medium to high heat. Add the eggplant circles and griddle for 2 to 3 minutes on each side until charred, then return to the marinade bowl and brush with any remaining sauce. Cover and keep warm in a low oven.

4. Add the soba noodles to a saucepan of boiling water and cook according to the package directions. Drain, rinse, and set aside.

5. Melt the coconut oil in a large skillet over medium to high heat. Add the onion, sprouts, and kale, season, and sauté for 2 to 3 minutes, or until starting to soften. Add 1½ tablespoons of the sauce and cook, stirring, for another 2 minutes.

6. Add the soba noodles and the remaining sauce to the pan, toss to combine, and heat through, then remove from the heat. Season to taste, adding another splash of tamari if needed, then top with the griddled eggplant, sprinkle over the cilantro and red pepper flakes, and serve.

BATTERED TOFU FINGERS

with salt & red pepper flakes

SERVES 4

If I had a cent for every time someone told me they hated tofu I'd be a very rich woman indeed. What I'd really like to do though is carry a batch of these with me everywhere I go, so I don't have to fruitlessly defend poor tofu's honor and can let the food do the talking instead. The crunchy batter that encases these beauties goes a very long way in showing bean curd off in its best possible light. It also happens to be gluten-free—curiously the coating doesn't work half as well with any other flour. Additional dietary requirements aside, if you're after a tofu recipe to win over dubious friends, may I kindly suggest that you have officially found it.

¾ cup rice flour

1 teaspoon gluten-free baking powder

½ teaspoon garlic powder

1 teaspoon sea salt flakes

1 teaspoon dried red pepper flakes

¼ teaspoon black pepper

1 heaping teaspoon brown or palm sugar

½ cup water

7 tablespoons olive oil

1 x 10½ oz firm tofu block, pressed (*see* page 11)

Salt and red pepper flake coating

1 heaping teaspoon fine sea salt

1 teaspoon dried red pepper flakes

¼ teaspoon light brown or palm sugar

¼ teaspoon black pepper

1. Put the rice flour, baking powder, garlic powder, sea salt, red pepper flakes, black pepper, and sugar in a mixing bowl. Stir to combine, then pour in the measured water and whisk to form a batter.

2. Heat the olive oil in a small skillet over medium to high heat to 350°F, or until a cube of bread browns in 30 seconds.

3. For the coating, put all the ingredients in a shallow bowl and mix to combine.

4. Cut the tofu block in half and slice the halves lengthwise into ¾ inch wide fingers. Dip each finger into the batter, then add them to pan in batches and fry in batches for 2 to 3 minutes on each side until golden, spooning a little more batter over the pieces before turning and being sure not to overcrowd the pan.

5. Remove the tofu pieces from the pan with tongs and drain on paper towels, then lightly dust with the salt and red pepper flake coating. Serve immediately.

FALAFEL SHAKSHUKA

SERVES 4

Falafel is a mainstay in many a vegan's weekly menu plan. A lunchtime fallback and perennial "we don't know what else to serve you" fave, it's become something of an unofficial running joke in vegan circles. I too was becoming a wee bit tired of consuming yet another falafel-and-salad-stuffed pita and honestly didn't believe "poaching" them would make that much difference. Or so I thought. Letting these chickpea-filled beauties steam until fluffy and virtually melt-in-the-mouth delicious in a sauce so good you'll be licking the pan was an absolute revelation. In fact, my love affair with these wondrous little veg-balls has officially been reignited—I'll never look at a falafel the same way again.

1 tablespoon olive oil
1 onion, finely chopped
1 small eggplant, sliced
3 garlic cloves, minced
1 scant teaspoon smoked paprika
¼ teaspoon ground cinnamon
1 tablespoon tomato paste
scant 1 cup strained tomatoes
2 cups canned chopped tomatoes
1 teaspoon dried red pepper flakes or 1 red chile, chopped
pinch of sugar
12 store-bought falafel
sea salt flakes and black pepper

Tahini sauce
2 tablespoons light tahini
½ tablespoon pomegranate molasses
1 teaspoon agave nectar
juice of ½ lemon
1 to 2 tablespoons water
pinch of fine sea salt flakes

To serve
8 to 10 taco-sized tortillas or flatbreads
handful of pomegranate seeds
handful of tarragon, torn

1. Heat the oil in a large skillet over medium heat. Add the onion to the pan, season, and sweat for 2 to 3 minutes until it begins to soften.

2. Add the eggplant and stir to combine. Sauté for 2 to 3 minutes, then add the garlic, sprinkle over the smoked paprika and cinnamon, and stir to coat. Cover and cook for another 2 to 3 minutes, or until the eggplant has started to soften.

3. Add the tomato paste, strained tomatoes, and chopped tomatoes to the pan. Fill the tomato can with water and add it to the sauce together with the red pepper flakes or chile and sugar. Season generously and simmer uncovered for about 20 minutes, or until the sauce is rich and bubbling.

4. Place the falafel in the pan, making sure not to cover them with the sauce—they should be peeking out! Cover and simmer gently for another 10 minutes.

5. Meanwhile, make the tahini sauce by whisking the ingredients together in a small bowl until smooth and glossy.

6. Griddle or toast the tortillas and keep warm under a clean dish towel.

7. To serve, drizzle the tahini sauce over the shakshuka and garnish with the pomegranate seeds and tarragon. Put the pan in the center of the table along with the tortillas and let everyone help themselves.

MY FAVORITE PENNE ALLA NORMA

SERVES 4

There are few things that give me more pleasure in life than a bowl of freshly cooked pasta, especially when paired with some sort of tomato sauce. In this case, I've opted for fresh tomatoes rather than canned, and I really think it makes a difference. Once simmered and reduced, this sauce is the perfect accompaniment to a simple dish of Sicilian origin—although I have to admit I have (a) never set foot in Sicily and (b) have zero claim to this being in any way authentic. I should be mortified but I'm not. In fact, I'm sure most Sicilians would recoil in horror at the very thought of "tofu ricotta," but once you get over that mental hurdle, you'll be able to fully appreciate what is really a rather lovely dish. Enjoy!

1 tablespoon olive oil
1 onion, sliced
1 eggplant, coarsely chopped
3 garlic cloves, minced
1 heaping teaspoon oregano
1 heaping tablespoon tomato paste
14 oz tomatoes, diced
1 large red chile, minced
1 tablespoon balsamic vinegar
1 cup water
10½ oz penne
1 tablespoon capers, minced
sea salt flakes and black pepper

Tofu ricotta
9 oz firm tofu
1 large garlic clove, grated
grated zest and juice of ½ lemon
3 tablespoons extra virgin olive oil
1 teaspoon sea salt flakes
black pepper

To serve
basil leaves, torn
extra virgin olive oil

1. To make the tofu ricotta, place all the ingredients in a food processor and pulse until everything is combined and the mixture has a smooth, ricottalike texture (be careful not to blend it too finely). Season to taste and refrigerate until needed.

2. Heat the olive oil in a large skillet over medium heat. Add the onion, season, and sweat for 4 to 5 minutes until softened and translucent.

3. Add the eggplant to the pan and sauté for 2 to 3 minutes until it begins to soften. Add the garlic, oregano, tomato paste, and a splash of water and cook, stirring, for another 1 to 2 minutes, then add the tomatoes, chile, balsamic vinegar, and measured water and simmer for 30 minutes, stirring occasionally, until the sauce has thickened and reduced.

4. Meanwhile, bring a large saucepan of salted water to a boil, add the penne, and cook for a few minutes under the recommended cooking time on the package. Drain and stir into the sauce with the capers, season with salt and pepper, and cook, stirring, for 5 minutes.

5. Remove from the heat and divide among bowls, spooning over the tofu ricotta, sprinkling over a few torn basil leaves, and drizzling generously with extra virgin olive oil to finish. Serve.

CURRIED CILANTRO PARSNIP SOUP

with roasted cashews

SERVES 2 TO 4

It always baffles (borderline offends) me when people tell me they think soup is boring. Perhaps it's my ultra-Irish upbringing but nothing manages to conjure up a better image of warmth and comfort to me than a steaming bowl of soup. This simple parsnip soup is spiked with just the right amount of spice to reenforce those well-entrenched memories … although granted, my childhood was less about curried anything and more about cream of tomato. Regardless, the sentiment remains the same and even though this recipe strays a little from tradition (roasted cashews will do that do a dish) this humble bowl has a reassuringly similar effect.

½ tablespoon coconut oil

1 small leek, trimmed, cleaned, and coarsely chopped

6 parsnips, peeled and chopped

2 garlic cloves, minced

1 thumb-sized piece of fresh ginger root, peeled and minced

1 teaspoon garam masala

1 teaspoon ground cumin

½ teaspoon mild curry powder

¼ teaspoon ground turmeric

¼ teaspoon cayenne powder (or chili powder)

½ tablespoon maple syrup

1 vegetable bouillon cube

1 kaffir lime leaf

3 cups water

large bunch of cilantro, chopped

sea salt flakes and black pepper

To serve

roasted cashews

chopped cilantro leaves

soy cream (optional)

1. Melt the coconut oil in a heavy saucepan over medium heat. Add the leek to the pan and sauté gently until slightly softened but not colored, then add the parsnips, garlic, and ginger. Cook, stirring, over low heat for 2 to 3 minutes, or until nicely aromatic.

2. Add the spices and maple syrup, stir to coat, and fry for another 2 to 3 minutes, then add the bouillon cube, lime leaf, and generous 2 cups of the water. Bring to a gentle simmer and cook for around 20 minutes, or until the parsnip is soft.

3. Remove and discard the lime leaf, transfer the soup to a blender or food processor with the chopped cilantro, and blend until completely smooth, then return the soup to the pan, add the remaining 1 cup water, and heat gently. Season to taste.

4. Serve in warmed bowls garnished with roasted cashews, chopped cilantro, and swirls of soy cream, if desired.

BLACK-EYED PEA STEW

with buckwheat pancakes & fried plantain

SERVES 2

I have a difficult relationship with buckwheat. I desperately want to love it but am often left feeling slightly underwhelmed. For this book I was determined to find a way to best utilize this naturally gluten-free grain (which is, somewhat confusingly, actually a seed) and these crêpe-like pancakes are the pleasing result. You can buy ready-ground buckwheat flour but I find grinding my own makes for a better crêpe—I also like to use buckwheat flakes in oatmeal, so tend to have them lying around. Getting these pancakes as thin as possible might take some practice. I find a rubber spatula helpful, letting me ease the batter to the edges of the pan. These pancakes also make terrific wraps, so if you have any left over, fill them with hummus and fresh veggies for lunch.

2 tablespoons olive oil
1 onion, sliced
1 celery stalk, sliced
1 red bell pepper, cored, seeded, and sliced
3 garlic cloves, minced
1 tablespoon red jalapeños, minced
1 heaping teaspoon chipotle paste
scant 1 cup canned coconut milk
1¾ cups canned black-eyed beans, drained and rinsed
sea salt flakes and black pepper

Buckwheat pancakes
scant ⅔ cup buckwheat flakes or flour

several thyme sprigs, leaves stripped
¼ teaspoon baking soda
juice of ½ lemon
⅔ to ¾ cup water
sea salt flakes and black pepper

Fried plantain
scant ¼ cup canola oil
1 large ripe plantain, sliced diagonally
¼ teaspoon sea salt flakes

To serve
1 ripe avocado, sliced
basil leaves, torn

1. For the pancakes, place the buckwheat, thyme leaves, and baking soda in a blender or food processor. Season and blitz until the mixture forms a fine flour, then transfer to a large mixing bowl, add the lemon juice and water, and whisk together to form a batter with the consistency of light cream. Set aside until needed.

2. Heat 1 tablespoon of the olive oil in a skillet over medium heat. Add the onion, celery, and red bell pepper, season, and fry until the vegetables begin to soften.

3. Add the garlic and jalapeños, stir to combine, and gently fry until aromatic, then stir in the chipotle paste and coconut milk. Season and bring to a gentle simmer. Cook for 10 minutes, then add the beans and simmer for another 5 minutes, or until the sauce has thickened and reduced. Cover with a lid and set aside.

4. Set a crepe pan over medium heat and brush it with 1 teaspoon of olive oil. Ladle a third of the batter into the pan and immediately spread it to the edges using a spatula, then cook for 3 to 4 minutes, or until the edges come away easily. Flip the pancake over and cook for another 30 seconds, then transfer to a dish and cover with a clean dish towel. Repeat until all the batter is used, adding another teaspoon or so of oil to the pan between each pancake.

5. To make the fried plantain, heat the canola oil in a skillet over medium to high heat, add the plantain slices, and fry for 2 to 3 minutes on each side until golden. Transfer to a plate lined with paper towels and sprinkle with sea salt.

6. To serve, fold the pancakes over crêpe suzette-style and top with the stew, fried plantain, sliced avocado, and torn basil leaves. Alternatively, fill and roll them up like fajitas, placing the individual dishes in the center of the table and letting everyone help themselves.

SWEET POTATO HASH BROWNS

with a chipotle sour cream

SERVES 2 TO 4

These sweet potato hash browns are seriously addictive. Piled high into the pan they soon reduce to a crispy mass of yumminess—a stripped back fritter, if you will. It helps to have a very wide spatula for flipping and make sure your pan is suitably nonstick to avoid any would-be disasters. Served alongside this smoky chipotle cashew cream they are a mega weekend treat that will be sure to become a firm brunch favorite.

2 large sweet potatoes, grated or spiralized
2 teaspoons ground cumin
1 teaspoon ground coriander
½ teaspoon ground cinnamon
1 to 1½ tablespoons coconut oil
sea salt flakes and black pepper
1 tablespoon chopped chives, to garnish

Chipotle sour cream
generous ¾ cup cashews, soaked and drained
(*see* page 8)
1 tablespoon cider vinegar
juice of ½ lemon
pinch of sea salt flakes
5 to 7 tablespoons water
1 tablespoon chipotle paste

1. For the chipotle sour cream, place the cashews in a blender along with the cider vinegar, lemon juice, salt, and 5 tablespoons of water. Blend until it is completely smooth, scraping down the sides periodically and adding a little more water if necessary. Once smooth, add the chipotle paste and blend to combine. Check for seasoning and refrigerate until needed.

2. Add the sweet potato and spices to a large mixing bowl, season with salt and pepper, and toss to combine.

3. Melt 1 heaping teaspoon of coconut oil in a skillet over medium heat. Add a large handful of the grated sweet potato mixture and press it down firmly using a spatula to form a rough circle. Repeat with a few more handfuls (you want to be careful not to overcrowd the pan, so it's best to cook these in batches). Fry for 5 minutes on each side, pressing down firmly on the hash browns with the spatula to help them bind together, until the edges begin to crisp.

4. Repeat until all the sweet potato has been used, adding a touch more coconut oil to the pan each time (the mixture should give around eight large hash browns). Divide among plates and serve immediately with a decent dollop of the chipotle sour cream and some chopped chives to garnish.

LIMA BEAN JALFREZI

SERVES 4

We all need a go-to weeknight meal and for me this is it. On the table in 30 minutes, it's rammed full of flavor and rates pretty well on the health-o-meter too. In many cases beans are interchangeable but I think these large circular lima bean disks add a meaty texture here that really can't be replicated with any other legume. I typically serve this with freshly boiled basmati but it would also be wonderful with any type of flatbread—both would be even better.

½ tablespoon coconut oil

1 celery stalk, minced

3 garlic cloves, minced

1 thumb-sized piece of fresh ginger root, peeled and minced

2 green chiles, minced

1 red bell pepper, cored, seeded, and coarsely chopped

1 yellow bell pepper, cored, seeded, and coarsely chopped

1 green bell pepper, cored, seeded, and coarsely chopped

1 heaping teaspoon garam masala

1 teaspoon ground cumin

½ teaspoon ground coriander

½ teaspoon ground turmeric

2 cups canned plum tomatoes

1 tablespoon tomato paste

1 teaspoon brown sugar

1 kaffir lime leaf (or bay leaf)

1⅓ cups canned lima beans, rinsed and drained

juice of ½ lime

3 tablespoons soy or coconut cream (optional)

sea salt flakes and black pepper

small bunch of cilantro, coarsely chopped, to garnish

basmati rice, to serve

1. Heat the coconut oil in a large saucepan over medium heat. Add the celery, garlic, ginger, and chile and fry gently until nicely aromatic.

2. Add the peppers to the pan, sprinkle over the spices, and season generously. Stir to coat then cook, stirring, for 2 to 3 minutes until the peppers begin to soften.

3. Add the tomatoes to the pan and break them up using the back of a spoon. Stir through the tomato paste and season generously, then add the sugar and lime leaf and bring to a gentle simmer. Cover and cook for 20 minutes, until the peppers are cooked through.

4. Stir in the lima beans and cook uncovered for another 10 minutes, or until the sauce has thickened and reduced. Add the lime juice and soy cream, if using, and simmer for another 1 to 2 minutes. Remove from the heat.

5. To serve, divide among bowls and sprinkle over the cilantro to garnish. Accompany with freshly boiled basmati rice.

EASY KOREAN RAMEN BOWL

SERVES 4

The success of this dish hinges entirely on the sauce. Who knew that peanut butter and gochujang (a fiery hot Korean paste) would be such a formidable pairing? I was so taken with it when I first discovered it that I made this dish (or a variation on it) every week for almost six months. Nothing could take the sheen off this number; I couldn't get enough. Should you wish to forgo the ramen element, feel free, because truthfully this recipe is also magnificent with steamed white rice—just don't put it underneath the sauce or else it will be swamped.

½ tablespoon coconut oil
1 red onion, coarsely chopped
1 large carrot, sliced diagonally
1 large parsnip, sliced diagonally
2 tablespoons gochujang (Korean chili paste)
1 tablespoon miso paste
1 tablespoon smooth peanut butter
½ tablespoon soy sauce, plus extra if needed
½ tablespoon maple syrup
6⅓ cups water
6 x 4 inch piece of kombu seaweed
handful of green beans, halved
½ head of cauliflower, broken into florets
3½ oz firm tofu, cut into cubes
9 oz fine rice noodle nests
sea salt flakes

Quick pickled cucumber
1 small cucumber, halved lengthwise and
    sliced into ribbons
½ tablespoon sugar
½ tablespoon sea salt flakes
juice of ½ lime (or lemon)
½ tablespoon Zingy Yuzu and Miso Dressing
    (see page 18)
1 teaspoon dried red pepper flakes
1 tablespoon black sesame seeds

To serve
2 scallions, sliced
small handful of cilantro leaves, coarsely
    chopped
1 nori seaweed sheet, shredded

1. To make the pickled cucumber, add the cucumber pieces to a shallow bowl, sprinkle over the sugar and salt, and pour over the lime juice and yuzu dressing. Toss to combine and set aside until needed.

2. Heat the coconut oil in a large heavy saucepan over medium heat. Add the onion, carrot, and parsnip to the pan, season with a little salt, and sauté for 1 to 2 minutes until slightly softened.

3. Add the gochujang, miso, smooth peanut butter, soy sauce, and maple syrup to the pan, pour over the measured water, and stir in the kombu.

4. Bring to the boil, then reduce the heat to a simmer and cook for 5 to 7 minutes. Remove the kombu and finely slice, then add to the pan with the beans and cauliflower and cook for another 10 minutes. Add the tofu and cook for 5 minutes to warm through. Season with salt, adding a splash of soy sauce if needed.

5. Divide the rice noodle nests among 4 deep bowls, then ladle over the stew so that the noodles are fully submerged. Leave the noodles for 2 to 3 minutes to soften in the broth before using chopsticks to break them up further and mix everything together thoroughly.

6. Stir the red pepper flakes and sesame seeds through the quick pickled cucumber and use it to top the ramen bowls together with the scallion, cilantro, and nori. Serve.

"CHIP-SHOP" VEGETABLE CURRY

SERVES 4

Anyone who grew up in the UK or Ireland will be familiar with that late-night takeout special, the incomparable "half and half" from the "chip shop". For those unfamiliar with the concept, it's a terribly inauthentic curry served with both rice and chunky French fries. Sounds vile, but after a heavy night on the tiles it's almost akin to salvation. You could say then that this is my homage to not only the curry that saved me from many a chronic hangover but also to those heady days that were wonderful at the time but which I have absolutely no desire to revisit.

1 tablespoon coconut oil	½ teaspoon ground coriander
1 onion, coarsely chopped	½ teaspoon ground turmeric
2 garlic cloves, minced	½ tablespoon palm or brown sugar
1 thumb-sized piece of fresh ginger root, peeled and minced	1 heaping tablespoon cornstarch
	generous 2 cups water
1 green chile, minced	1 heaping tablespoon tomato paste
7 oz mushrooms, trimmed and sliced	2 kaffir lime leaves
½ head of cauliflower, broken into small florets	scant 1 cup canned coconut milk
	⅔ cup frozen peas
1 heaping teaspoon garam masala	3½ oz spinach, blanched and chopped
1 teaspoon ground cumin	sea salt flakes and black pepper

1. Heat the coconut oil in a large pan over medium heat. Add the onion, season with salt and pepper, and sweat for 3 to 4 minutes, until translucent.

2. Add the garlic, ginger, and chile to the pan and sauté for 2 to 3 minutes, or until aromatic.

3. Add the mushrooms to the pan, season generously, and cook over medium to high heat for 5 minutes, or until the mushrooms begin to color, release their juices, and shrink.

4. Add the cauliflower florets to the pan together with the spices, sugar, and a splash of water. Cook for 1 to 2 minutes before sprinkling over the cornstarch and stirring to coat evenly.

5. Pour over the measured water and stir continuously until the sauce thickens, then add the tomato paste and lime leaves.

6. Bring to a simmer, cover, and let cook for 20 minutes, then stir in the coconut milk, peas, and spinach. Season generously and simmer for another 10 to 15 minutes, uncovered, until thickened and reduced. Season to taste and serve.

SWEET 'N' STICKY CAULIFLOWER FLORETS

with a cooling coconut dip

SERVES 4

Whether it's griddled, baked, or even blitzed into "rice," I've found a multitude of uses for cauliflower but none of them have quite had that "knock-yer-socks-off" effect that this one possesses. Gochujang may seem like a specialty ingredient but thankfully it's now widely available in grocery stores. I guarantee this spicy Korean paste will soon become a staple—I like to dollop it into stews to boost flavor. Think of this as the ultimate cauliflower dish that'll have you coming back for more.

1⅔ cups panko bread crumbs
1 head of cauliflower, broken into florets

Batter
½ cup gram (chickpea) or rice flour
pinch of sea salt flakes
¼ teaspoon garlic powder
¼ teaspoon white pepper
¼ teaspoon baking soda
juice of ½ lemon
⅔ cup soy milk

Gochujang dressing
2 heaping tablespoons gochujang (Korean red chili paste)

2 tablespoons soy sauce
1 tablespoon cider (or rice wine) vinegar
3 tablespoons maple syrup
scant ¼ cup water, plus extra if necessary

Cooling coconut dipping sauce
⅔ cup coconut yogurt
1 garlic clove, minced
grated zest and juice of 1 lemon
1 teaspoon cider vinegar
pinch of pink Himalayan salt or sea salt flakes

To serve
½ cucumber, finely sliced
1 tablespoon black sesame seeds

1. Preheat the oven to 475°F and line a baking sheet with aluminum foil or parchment paper.

2. Place the ingredients for the coconut dipping sauce in a blender and blitz together until smooth (alternatively, vigorously whisk them together in a bowl until combined). Refrigerate until needed.

3. To make the batter, whisk the ingredients together in a bowl until smooth.

4. Place the panko bread crumbs in a food processor and pulse briefly to break up any large pieces. Transfer to a separate bowl.

5. Dip a cauliflower floret first in the batter and shake off any excess before dredging in the panko crumbs and placing on the prepared baking sheet. Repeat with the rest of the florets, then bake for 25 minutes, turning once, until crispy and golden.

6. Meanwhile, place the gochujang dressing ingredients in a saucepan, bring to a boil, and cook for 2 to 3 minutes, or until smooth and glossy, adding a splash more water if the dressing looks as though it is getting too thick. Keep warm over low heat.

7. Transfer the baked cauliflower to a large bowl, pour over the dressing, and toss to coat, then sprinkle over the cucumber slices and sesame seeds to finish. Serve with the coconut dipping sauce.

SPICE IT UP!

HARISSA-COATED TOFU KEBABS

SERVES 4

If you're of the common opinion that tofu is bland then this is absolutely the recipe to change your mind. It's funny how a handful of familiar ingredients can transform a slab of bean curd into something even your average meat-eater would devour (no mean feat, I can tell you), although be prepared for the predictable round of tofu jokes. I'm fairly certain I've heard them all by this stage. Harissa paste is a trusty staple in my pantry and is made for marinades, in my opinion. Here it is an absolute godsend, raising the tofu bar to next-level greatness and rendering most naysayers speechless in the process. I love the "popsicle" kitschness of the skewers, which helps make them a must-have at any summer barbecue, served alongside a bounty of sides and salads. Vegan or not, these are sure to be a fiery hit.

**(1) 14 oz firm tofu block, pressed
(see page 11)
2 tablespoons harissa paste
juice of ½ lemon**

**1 tablespoon olive oil
½ tablespoon agave nectar
pinch of sea salt flakes**

1. Cut the tofu block in half and slice the halves lengthwise into ¾ inch wide fingers.

2. Combine the harissa, lemon juice, oil, agave nectar, and salt in a shallow bowl and whisk vigorously to combine. Add the tofu to the bowl and turn to coat, then transfer to the refrigerator and let marinate for 1 to 2 hours.

3. Heat a ridged grill pan or barbecue to medium to high. Gently push a bamboo skewer through each of the tofu fingers, transfer to the awaiting grill pan or barbecue and cook for 5 to 7 minutes on each side until nicely charred.

4. Brush over any remaining marinade and serve with a salad.

TABASCO-DRENCHED TOMATOES

SERVES 4

I have such fondness for roasted tomatoes. They can be served with a multitude of dishes but I prefer them simply on freshly toasted bread—slices of nutty rye are especially good. I like to cut them into wedges, not only because they are easier to eat but also because there's more surface area to carry the array of in-your-face flavors. I've called for one teaspoon of Tabasco sauce in this recipe, but if I'm being totally honest I usually add a touch more. If you think you're brave enough (and after all, they really should be "drenched" in Tabasco) then I heartily recommend two.

3 large tomatoes
6 garlic cloves
1 tablespoon tamari
1 tablespoon balsamic vinegar
1 tablespoon olive oil

½ tablespoon date syrup
1 teaspoon Tabasco sauce
pinch of dried red pepper flakes
sea salt flakes and black pepper
rye bread, to serve

1. Preheat the oven to 425°F.

2. Cut the tomatoes into wedges and place them in an ovenproof dish along with the garlic cloves in their skins.

3. Drizzle the tamari, balsamic vinegar, olive oil, date syrup, and Tabasco over the tomatoes, season with salt and pepper, and sprinkle over the red pepper flakes. Roast for 30 minutes until wrinkled and lightly browned.

4. Serve the tomatoes on top of thick slices of toasted rye bread spread with the roasted garlic, squeezed from its skins.

SPICY MUSHROOM-STUFFED CALZONE

MAKES 4

What's better than a pizza? A pizza that has been stuffed, folded, and crimped, of course! And filled with spicy, creamy mushrooms? Even better. There are several elements to this recipe, putting it in the "at your leisure" category—that is, one of those dishes best reserved for a quiet weekend rather than a manic Tuesday evening. Of course, you could also make the dough ahead of time, and thankfully these calzones also reheat well too. If I want to serve them at gatherings, I bake them until cooked but not crispy and then finish them off in a hot oven when my guests arrive.

1 teaspoon instant yeast
scant ⅔ cup warm water
1 tablespoon olive oil
1 tablespoon agave nectar or maple syrup
1⅔ cups all-purpose flour
1 heaping teaspoon sea salt flakes

Mushrooms
1 tablespoon olive oil
10½ oz cremini mushrooms, trimmed and
   coarsely chopped
1 green chile, chopped
1 garlic clove, minced
3 scallions, sliced
1 x Cashew Sour Cream (*see* page 10)
sea salt flakes and black pepper

1. Add the yeast and warm water to a pitcher, stir, and set aside for 10 minutes until foaming, then add the oil and agave nectar and whisk lightly to combine.

2. Place the flour and salt in a large mixing bowl or stand mixer, gradually add the yeast mixture and mix together to form a rough dough. Turn the dough out on to a floured counter and knead for 10 minutes until smooth and elastic, then return it to the bowl with a little oil, cover with a clean dish towel, and leave in a warm place to rise for up to 2 hours, or until doubled in size.

3. For the mushrooms, heat the olive oil in a large skillet over medium to high heat. Add the mushrooms to the pan, season, and sauté until they release their juices and begin to soften, about 5 to 7 minutes. Add the chile and garlic and cook for another 5 minutes, then stir through the scallions, season generously, and cook over low heat for an additional 1 to 2 minutes. Pour over the cashew cream and gently heat through. Once the sauce has thickened slightly, take the pan off the heat and let cool.

4. Preheat the oven to its highest setting—usually around 525°F—and place an upturned baking sheet on to the top shelf (this will act as your pizza stone).

5. Tip the dough on to a floured counter and knead lightly a few times before dividing into four even-sized pieces. Shape each piece into a ball before rolling out into rough oval shapes. Divide the mushroom and cashew cream mixture among the ovals, placing it on one side of the dough only, then fold the dough over and crimp the edges using wetted fingertips to seal in the filling. Lightly dust each calzone with a little flour.

6. Lightly dust the preheated baking sheet with flour, then transfer the calzone to the tray and bake for 20 to 25 minutes, or until the calzone begin to brown and crisp. Serve immediately.

GRAINS & GOODNESS

QUINOA-STUFFED TOMATOES

SERVES 4 TO 6

Tomatoes might be my favorite fruit. Endlessly versatile, they are an absolute mainstay in my kitchen and, whether canned or fresh, they form the basis of so many of my meals. Here though they really get to shine, becoming the vehicles for a simple but tasty quinoa filling. These stuffed tomatoes can be wheeled out for an easy lunch or served as part of a potluck dinner or buffet—tasting equally wonderful cold as fresh out of the oven makes them a great option for stress-free hosting. For a rather adorable (and delicious) appetizer, serve them nestled on top of some dressed leaves.

½ cup quinoa (any color)

scant 1 cup water

2 tablespoons olive oil

1 red onion, minced

1 zucchini, diced

grated zest and juice of ½ lemon

¾ cup fresh or frozen corn kernels

scant ½ cup frozen peas, defrosted

1 heaping tablespoon vegan pesto,
    homemade (*see* page 141) or store-bought

scant ¼ cup chopped cashews

6 large tomatoes

sea salt flakes and black pepper

To serve

small handful of mint, chopped

small handful of flat-leaf parsley, chopped

1. Add the quinoa to a saucepan and pour over the measured water. Cover with a lid and bring to a boil, then reduce the heat to a simmer and cook for 8 to 10 minutes, or until all the liquid has been absorbed. Remove from the heat and let steam, covered, for 5 minutes, then fluff the quinoa grains up with a fork and set aside (this can be prepared up to a day in advance and kept in a suitable container in the refrigerator until needed).

2. Preheat the oven to 425°F.

3. Heat 1 tablespoon of the olive oil in a skillet over medium heat. Add the onion, season generously, and sweat for 4 to 5 minutes until translucent. Add the zucchini and lemon zest and cook, stirring, for 5 to 7 minutes until the zucchini begins to soften.

4. Stir through the quinoa, corn, peas, and lemon juice and season. Cook for 2 to 3 minutes to heat through before stirring through the pesto and cashews. Remove from the heat.

5. Use a sharp knife to cut the tops from the tomatoes (being sure to set them aside) and hollow out the seeds and membranes using a spoon.

6. Spoon the quinoa mixture into the tomatoes, pressing down gently on the filling as you go. Transfer to a baking dish, pop the tops back on, drizzle with the remaining olive oil, and season.

7. Bake for 20 minutes until lightly charred and blistered, then remove from the oven and set aside for 5 minutes to cool slightly. Divide among plates and garnish with a little chopped mint and parsley. Serve.

SUMMERY SPELT SALAD

with roasted cauliflower & grapes

SERVES 4

I don't use spelt enough. However, each time I make this dish I'm reminded how much I adore this wonderful grain. If you have never roasted grapes before, you'll be surprised at how magnificent they are all blistered and bruised and bursting with flavor. I really should do it more often.

1 cup spelt grains, soaked overnight and rinsed

½ large cucumber, cut into ribbons

2 tablespoons cider vinegar

1 tablespoon agave nectar

½ teaspoon sea salt flakes

small bunch of dill, finely chopped, plus extra torn fronds to serve

handful of pomegranate seeds, to garnish

Roasted cauliflower & grapes

1 small head of cauliflower, broken into florets

1 tablespoon olive oil

1 heaping teaspoon za'atar (or dried thyme)

⅓ cup seedless black grapes

Dressing

½ cup sunflower seeds

⅔ to ¾ cup water

1 teaspoon Dijon mustard

juice of ½ lemon

½ tablespoon pomegranate molasses

½ tablespoon agave nectar or maple syrup

sea salt flakes and black pepper

1. Add the spelt grains to a large saucepan and pour over 3 cups water. Cover and bring to a boil, then reduce the heat to a simmer and cook for 1 to 1¼ hours, or until all the liquid has been absorbed. Remove from the heat and let steam, covered, for 5 to 10 minutes, then fluff the grains up with a fork and set aside to cool completely.

2. Preheat the oven to 425°F.

3. Put the cauliflower florets in a bowl with the olive oil, toss to coat, and sprinkle over the za'atar. Season generously, arrange on a baking sheet in an even layer and roast for 15 minutes, then add the grapes and roast for 5 minutes, or until the cauliflower is lightly charred and the grapes are blistered.

4. Meanwhile, put the cucumber ribbons in a bowl. Whisk the cider vinegar, agave nectar, and salt together in a separate bowl, then pour over the cucumber ribbons and set aside for 15 to 20 minutes to lightly pickle.

5. Place the cooled spelt in a shallow serving bowl together with a tablespoon or so of the cucumber pickling liquid. Drain the cucumber, add it to the bowl with the dill, and toss everything together with your hands to combine.

6. To make the dressing, place all the ingredients in a blender and blitz until completely smooth, scraping down the sides from time to time as you go.

7. To serve, top the salad with the roasted cauliflower and grapes, drizzle over the dressing, and garnish with the pomegranate seeds and a few torn dill fronds to finish.

MEGA MISO FREEKEH BOWL

SERVES 2

Miso is a miracle worker when it comes to injecting serious flavor. If ever I'm in search of that extra something, I know that a little piece of this salty paste will come to the rescue and knock it right out of the park. If you can't get your hands on smoked freekeh (or even freekeh for that matter) don't panic—the arguably more accessible bulgur wheat will do an equally fine job. There's always a solution to any food-related problem. Just don't omit the miso.

½ tablespoon coconut oil
½ red onion, minced
scant 1 cup smoked freekeh (or bulgur wheat)
2 tablespoons miso paste
generous 2 cups water
1 large carrot, grated
1 large parsnip, grated
3½ oz kale, leaves torn and stems removed
juice of ½ lemon

2 large medjool dates, pitted and chopped
1 tablespoon toasted peanuts
sea salt flakes and black pepper

To serve
7 oz steamed purple sprouting broccoli
1 x "Goes-with-Everything" Tahini Sauce
   (see page 151)

1. Melt the oil in a large skillet over medium heat. Add the onion, season, and sauté for 4 to 5 minutes until softened and slightly colored.

2. Add the freekeh and miso paste to the pan, pour over the measured water, and stir gently until the paste has dissolved. Bring to a simmer and cook, uncovered and stirring occasionally, for 20 to 25 minutes, or until most of the liquid has been absorbed and the grains are tender but still retaining some bite.

3. Add the carrot and parsnip to the pan, stir to combine, and cover with a lid. Reduce the heat to low and cook gently for 1 to 2 minutes, then stir in the kale and lemon juice and cook, covered, for another 2 to 3 minutes until the kale is wilted.

4. Remove from the heat and stir through the dates and peanuts, then divide between bowls. Serve with steamed broccoli and my "goes-with-everything" tahini sauce.

CAJUN KIDNEY BEAN & BROWN RICE BROTH

I had previously entitled this simple bowl of goodness "Soothing Kidney Bean & Brown Rice Broth" because it has a curiously Zen-like ability to rectify even the most stressful of days. I love the smoky heat from the paprika and cayenne combo, which provides just enough kick without being too overpowering. This is bowl food for the soul with the added bonus of being an absolute cinch to make. I like to make a batch at the start of the week and dip into it for lunch or dinner, or alternatively freeze it and reheat servings as and when needed. It also makes a terrific, warming appetizer for any laid-back gathering—simply ladle into mugs and serve.

1 tablespoon olive oil
1 red onion, minced
3 garlic cloves, minced
1 red chile, minced
¼ teaspoon cayenne pepper
¼ teaspoon garlic powder
1 teaspoon ground cumin
1 teaspoon smoked paprika
scant 1 cup strained tomatoes
4 cups vegetable broth
1 cup brown rice

2½ cups canned kidney beans, rinsed
   and drained
3½ oz kale, leaves torn and stems removed
½ tablespoon balsamic vinegar
sea salt flakes and black pepper

To serve
1 ripe avocado, sliced
handful of salad cress
a few splashes of Tabasco sauce

1.   Heat the olive oil in a heavy saucepan over low heat. Add the onion to the pan, season, and sauté for 5 minutes until beginning to soften, then add the garlic and chile and sauté for another 3 to 4 minutes, or until the onion becomes translucent.

2.   Mix the spices together in a small bowl, add them to the pan, and stir to coat. Pour over the strained tomatoes and vegetable broth and bring to a boil, then add the brown rice and reduce to a gentle simmer. Cook for 30 minutes, or until the rice is cooked through.

3.   Add the kidney beans, kale, and balsamic vinegar to the pan and cook for another 10 minutes, or until the kale wilts. Season to taste.

4.   Divide the broth among bowls and top each with a few avocado slices, some salad cress, and a splash of Tabasco before serving.

WARMING RED PEPPER SOUP

with crispy polenta wedges

SERVES 4

Perhaps it's because I'm a sucker for all things soup that this is up there with some of my favorite dishes, though there's something about this piercingly hot red pepper number coupled with the perfectly seasoned crisp polenta wedges that makes it a dish to remember. Even though this dish has an air of winter about it, my best memory attached to it (yes, I have an embarrassingly catalog-like recollection for "when," "where," and "with whom" I ate certain foods) involves sitting outside on a searing hot summer's day with new friends and lots of laughter. Such a simple dish and a simple moment, but so lovely too.

1 tablespoon olive oil

2 small onions, chopped

4 garlic cloves, minced

5 large red bell peppers, cored, seeded, and
coarsely chopped

1 heaping tablespoon tomato paste

scant 1 cup strained tomatoes

¼ teaspoon Tabasco sauce

1 tablespoon maple syrup

generous 2 cups water

sea salt flakes and black pepper

scant ¼ cup tablespoon coarsely chopped
curly parsley, to garnish

Crispy polenta wedges

3 cups water

1 vegetable bouillon cube

⅓ cup cornmeal

juice of ½ lemon

2 tablespoons olive oil

1 teaspoon dried red pepper flakes

sea salt flakes and black pepper

1. Line a 12 x 8 inch brownie pan with parchment paper.

2. For the polenta wedges, bring the measured water to a boil in a large saucepan. Add the bouillon cube and stir to dissolve, then gradually whisk in the cornmeal and reduce the heat to low simmer. Cook, stirring continuously, for 15 to 20 minutes, or until the cornmeal becomes thick and rubbery, then stir in the lemon juice and 1 tablespoon of the olive oil. Remove from the heat and spoon into the prepared pan, spreading it out evenly to the edges with a spatula. Cover with plastic wrap and refrigerate for 2 to 3 hours, or until firm.

3. Heat the olive oil in a heavy saucepan over low heat. Add the onions, season, and sweat for 2 to 3 minutes until they begin to soften, then stir in the garlic and sauté for another 5 to 7 minutes, or until the onion is translucent.

4. Add the chopped peppers to the pan, season generously with salt and pepper, and sauté for 2 to 3 minutes, then add the tomato paste, strained tomatoes, Tabasco, maple syrup, and measured water. Season again and bring to a gentle simmer, then cover with a lid and cook for 20 to 25 minutes, or until the peppers are soft.

5. Transfer the mixture to a blender or food processor and blend until completely smooth, then return the mixture to the pan. Keep warm.

6. Remove the polenta from the refrigerator and slice it into eighths before halving each slice diagonally into triangles.

7. Heat a ridged grill pan over medium to high heat and lightly brush it with the remaining oil. Add the polenta wedges and cook for 3 to 4 minutes on each side until crispy, golden, and lightly marked. Transfer to a dish, sprinkle over the red pepper flakes, and season to taste.

8. Check the soup for seasoning before dividing among warmed bowls, adding a couple of polenta wedges and a sprinkling of parsley to each before serving.

EGGPLANT INVOLTINI

with a bulgur wheat & couscous filling

SERVES 4

Fiddly? Tick. Worth it? Absolutely. OK, so you're probably not going to make this often but that's fine, because there's a place for special dishes in our repertoire too—I sometimes earmark this one for a Sunday when I have a bit more time. The good news is that you can make the involtini in advance and refrigerate them until needed (just be sure not to add the sauce until you're just about to bake this dish, otherwise it will be absorbed into the rolls). I always think this impressively rustic dish looks like it was made with love, which is never a bad thing when you're feeding friends.

3 tablespoons olive oil
2 large eggplants, cut lengthwise into
   ½ inch thick slices
sea salt flakes and black pepper

small bunch of fresh basil, finely chopped
small bunch of flat-leaf parsley, finely
   chopped
sea salt flakes and black pepper

Bulgur wheat & couscous filling
½ cup bulgur wheat
½ cup couscous
1 heaping teaspoon ground cumin
1 teaspoon fine sea salt flakes
approx. 1 cup boiling water
juice of 1 lemon
⅓ cup toasted pine nuts
⅓ cup golden raisins or raisins

Spicy tomato sauce
1 tablespoon olive oil
3 garlic cloves, minced
1 cup canned tomatoes
scant 1 cup strained tomatoes
⅔ cup water
1 teaspoon chili powder
1 tablespoon maple syrup
sea salt flakes and black pepper

1.   Preheat the oven to 425°F.
2.   For the tomato sauce, heat the olive oil in a large saucepan over medium heat, add the garlic, and sauté for 2 to 3 minutes, or until aromatic. Add the tomatoes, strained tomatoes, and measured water and stir to combine, breaking up any large pieces of tomato with the back of a spoon. Stir in the chili powder and maple syrup, season generously, and simmer for 30 to 40 minutes until the sauce is thick and glossy, then remove from the heat and set aside.
3.   Meanwhile, set a ridged grill pan over medium to high heat and lightly brush with a little olive oil. Brush the eggplant slices with a little more oil and griddle in batches for 3 to 4 minutes on each side until charred and marked. Transfer to a dish, season lightly, and let cool.
4.   For the filling, place the bulgur wheat, couscous, cumin, and salt in a large mixing bowl and toss to combine. Pour enough boiling water over the grains to just cover, then cover with plastic wrap or a plate. Set aside for 15 to 20 minutes, until the water has been completely absorbed, before fluffing up with a fork and stirring through the lemon juice, pine nuts, golden raisins, and herbs. Check for seasoning.

5. Ladle a third of the sauce over the bottom of a 12 x 8 inch baking dish. Take a slice of griddled eggplant and place a spoonful of the bulgur wheat filling in the center at the widest part, then carefully roll it up to form a neat little bundle. Transfer to the baking dish and repeat until all the eggplant slices have been filled (you can serve any leftover filling alongside the dish or keep it for a lunch).

6. Spoon the remaining sauce evenly over the involtini, cover with foil, and bake for 25 minutes before removing the foil and returning to the oven for another 15 minutes until lightly golden and bubbling. Remove from the oven and let cool slightly before serving alongside a crisp green salad.

MIXED PEPPER CAPONATA

with capers & popped quinoa

SERVES 2 TO 4

If I had to pick one salad to eat for the entirety of the summer then this is the one I would choose. In truth, I've been making variations on caponata for years now and I'm not even close to tiring of it. It's often the one dish I will bring to a barbecue because it requires the least explaining and has a way of covering most dietary requirements—dairy-free, gluten-free, you name it. There's something uniquely wonderful that happens to a pepper when roasted—in fact, I'm not sure there's a greater vegetable transformation to be found. Never have I come across such a universally pleasing dish—not even the remnants of the dressing are safe, just you wait and see. It's no wonder it's become a crucial part of my recipe armor, and I really hope it'll become part of yours, too.

1 large red bell pepper, cored, seeded, and cut into quarters

1 large green bell pepper, cored, seeded, and cut into quarters

1 large yellow bell pepper, cored, seeded, and cut into quarters

scant ¼ cup quinoa (any color or a mixture), rinsed and dried

1 teaspoon baby capers

Dressing

large handful fresh basil

1 large garlic clove

2 teaspoons baby capers

pinch of sea salt flakes

3 tablespoons balsamic vinegar

2 tablespoons extra virgin olive oil

juice of ½ lemon

½ tablespoon agave nectar (or maple syrup or brown sugar)

black pepper

1. Preheat a broiler to high.

2. Arrange the pepper quarters skin-side up on a baking sheet, place under the hot broiler, and cook for 8 to 10 minutes, or until the skins are black and blistered. Transfer to a bowl, wrap in plastic wrap, and let cool, then peel the skins off and cut the flesh into thick ribbons. Transfer to a shallow serving dish.

3. Heat a cast-iron skillet with a lid until it begins to smoke. Tip the quinoa into the pan, turn the heat down to medium. and cover with the lid. Cook for 1 to 2 minutes, shaking the pan as you go and checking on the quinoa from time to time to ensure it isn't burning, until the quinoa has popped. Remove from the heat and transfer to a baking sheet to cool.

4. For the dressing, place the basil, garlic, capers, and salt in a mortar and pestle and grind to a coarse paste. Add the balsamic vinegar, oil, lemon juice, and agave nectar, season generously, and mix together vigorously until it emulsifies.

5. Drizzle the dressing over the peppers and sprinkle over the popped quinoa and capers. Serve.

WASABI-DUSTED POPCORN

SERVES 4 TO 6

Popcorn is my perennial snack of choice. Granted, my husband is the designated "popper" while I am the "coater"—that is, he does all the hard work and I get to pretty it up at the end. Story of my (or should I say his) life. My current flavor kick is a combination of coconut butter (yes, coconut oil will do at a pinch) and a generous dusting of palm sugar, wasabi, and salt in almost equal proportions. The oven stage is optional but I feel that having been coated with butter and/or oil, the once-crisp popcorn needs to regain its form again, so it's worth the extra effort.

1 teaspoon wasabi powder

1 tablespoon palm sugar

½ teaspoon pink Himalayan salt

1 teaspoon coconut oil

½ cup popcorn kernels

3½ tablespoons coconut butter

1. Preheat the oven to 400°F. Line a baking sheet with parchment paper.
2. Combine the wasabi powder, palm sugar, and salt in a bowl and set aside until needed.
3. Heat the coconut oil in a large heavy saucepan over medium to high heat. Add a couple of popcorn kernels initially to test the temperature—as soon as they begin to pop, add the remaining kernels and clamp on the lid. Once the kernels begin to pop more vigorously, shake the pan to ensure they all reach the heat evenly, and when the popping slows to just a few pops here and there, it's time to take the pan off the heat and tip the popcorn into a bowl.
4. Meanwhile, gently melt the coconut butter a little in a separate saucepan (it doesn't need to be completely liquefied, as the hot popcorn will melt it further). If it starts to brown a little, simply take it off the heat and give it a good stir.
5. Pour the coconut butter over the popcorn along with half the wasabi powder mixture and mix it together with a wooden spoon or spatula, ensuring all the kernels are coated.
6. Transfer the popcorn to the prepared baking sheet, sprinkle over the remaining wasabi powder mixture, and stir to combine, then pop in the oven for 8 to 10 minutes until crunchy and golden. Remove from the oven and let cool before serving. Any leftover popcorn will keep stored in an airtight container for up to 3 days.

PEARL BARLEY PAELLA

with paprika-roasted tempeh

SERVES 4

Tempeh isn't something I eat a tremendous amount of although I do favor its inclusion here. Tossed in smoked paprika and a touch of sugar (don't omit it) and roasted until golden (or as golden as tempeh gets), it does have the ability to bring this dish together. I often use pearl barley in place of rice when making paella and I adore its inimitable chew—it might not be authentic but it's certainly damned delicious, so you'll be getting no apologies from me. Served this dish with a glass of chilled wine, I could almost be forgiven for thinking I'm dining on the Costa Brava in Spain. Either that or my finely tuned imagination is wreaking havoc with reality again. Probably the latter.

1 tablespoon olive oil
1 onion, minced
1 celery stalk, finely chopped
1 carrot, finely chopped
3 garlic cloves, minced
grated zest and juice of ½ lemon
1 teaspoon smoked paprika
generous 1 cup pearl barley
4 cups vegetable broth
2 to 3 saffron threads
2 cups canned chopped tomatoes
1 bay leaf
3½ oz green beans, chopped
scant ½ cup frozen peas

Paprika-roasted tempeh
1 teaspoon smoked paprika
½ teaspoon garlic powder
pinch of brown sugar
3 tablespoons olive oil
5¼ oz tempeh, cubed
sea salt flakes and black pepper

To serve
¼ cup sunflower seeds
small handful of flat-leaf parsley, coarsely chopped
1 lemon, cut into wedges

1.   Preheat the oven to 425°F.

2.   Heat the oil in a large deep skillet over medium heat. Add the onion, celery, and carrot to the pan, season, and sweat for 3 to 4 minutes, or until the vegetables begin to soften.

3.   Add the garlic, lemon zest, and paprika to the pan and sauté for 1 to 2 minutes, or until aromatic. Stir through the pearl barley, add the broth, saffron, tomatoes, and bay leaf, bring to a simmer, and cook for 50 minutes, stirring occasionally, until the pearl barley grains are tender but retain some bite.

4.   Meanwhile, make the tempeh. Combine the smoked paprika, garlic powder, sugar, and oil in a bowl, add the tempeh, and toss together. Season with salt and pepper and roast for 25 minutes, or until browned.

5.   Add the green beans to the paella and cook for another 10 minutes, adding the peas a few minutes before the end. Squeeze over the lemon juice and season to taste, then remove from the heat and top with the roasted tempeh pieces. Garnish with sunflower seeds, coarsely chopped flat-leaf parsley, and lemon wedges before serving.

PUY LENTIL RAGU

with homemade tagliatelle

SERVES 4

Everyone and their granny has their own definitive answer to the vegan ragu recipe question. And while I do waiver between red and green lentils, the green win out because they can stand up to more vigorous simmering without dissolving into mush. Perhaps the most satisfying ribbons of loveliness I have ever created, the homemade tagliatelle are worth every second of rolling and rerolling.

1 tablespoon olive oil

1 red onion, finely chopped

1 carrot, finely chopped

1 celery stalk, finely chopped

1 cup mushrooms, finely chopped

4 garlic cloves, minced

1 heaping teaspoon dried oregano

generous ¾ cup Puy lentils, rinsed and drained

½ cup vegan red wine

1 heaping tablespoon tomato paste

2 cups canned tomatoes

⅔ cup strained tomatoes

1 tablespoon balsamic vinegar

½ tablespoon yeast extract or liquid seasoning

1 teaspoon brown or palm sugar

1¾ cups water

1 bay leaf

sea salt flakes and black pepper

Pasta

3 cups "00" pasta flour, plus extra for dusting

1 teaspoon sea salt flakes

generous 1 cup water

1 tablespoon olive oil

1. For the pasta, place the flour and salt in a food processor and pulse to combine. Whisk the water and oil together and gradually add to the flour, pulsing continuously, until the mixture forms a rough dough ball. Turn out onto a clean counter and knead for 1 minute, then wrap in plastic wrap, transfer to the refrigerator, and let rest for 1 to 2 hours.

2. Heat the olive oil in a large skillet over medium heat. Add the onion, carrot, and celery, season, cover and sweat for 5 to 7 minutes, until the vegetables begin to soften. Add the mushrooms and cook for a further 2 to 3 minutes until softened.

3. Add the garlic, oregano, and Puy lentils to the pan and cook, stirring, for 1 to 2 minutes, until the aromas begin to exude. Pour in the red wine, increase the heat to high, and cook until the wine has evaporated.

4. Stir in the tomato paste, then add the canned tomatoes, strained tomatoes, balsamic vinegar, yeast extract, sugar, and measured water. Season generously, add the bay leaf, and simmer for at least 1 hour, stirring frequently, until the lentils are cooked and the sauce is thick and glossy.

5. Roll the pasta dough out on a lightly floured counter until it is almost transparent, turning it frequently so it doesn't stick. Using a sharp knife, cut the dough into tagliatelle-sized strips. (alternatively, use a pasta maker if you have one.) Dust the ribbons with flour to prevent sticking.

6. Bring a large pan of salted water to a boil, add the pasta to the pan, and cook for 3 to 4 minutes until al dente. Drain and divide between warmed bowls, top with the ragu, and serve.

SWEET POTATO & WALNUT KOFTAS

MAKES 12

Walnuts are a wonder—and I'm not just talking about their omega-3 content, although I'll admit that is something of a draw. For me, vegan meatballs, burgers, and anything else of that ilk can be a little underwhelming, with a tendency to fall apart at first bite. I know you know what I mean. This is where the humble walnut (with a little help from the ever-reliable sweet potato) comes in. Not only do walnuts add bite and texture but, crucially, they help form a surprisingly "meaty" ball with the added bonus of being, well, good for you. However you shape them, these koftas are guaranteed to be devoured, whether served as finger food at parties (with requisite spicy dip accompaniment), stuffed into pitas loaded with salad, avocado, and hummus (standard) or even doused in a rich tomato sauce for a twist on meatballs and spaghetti (my preference, if anyone's asking). Certified winners, whichever way you go.

1 small sweet potato, halved

2 tablespoons olive oil

1 tablespoon milled flaxseed

1 cup lightly toasted walnuts

generous 1 cup panko bread crumbs

1 teaspoon dried oregano

1 teaspoon ground cumin

½ teaspoon ground coriander

¼ teaspoon ground cinnamon

½ teaspoon dried red pepper flakes

small bunch of cilantro, coarsely chopped

1 scallion, very finely chopped

sea salt flakes and black pepper

1. Preheat the oven to 425°F.

2. Lightly brush the sweet potato halves with 1 teaspoon of the olive oil, arrange skin-side down on a baking sheet, and bake for 40 minutes until soft. Remove from the oven, scoop out the flesh into a bowl, and season lightly. Let cool.

3. Combine the flaxseed with 3 tablespoons water. Set aside for 5 to 10 minutes.

4. Place the walnuts in a processor and pulse to a fine crumb. Add the bread crumbs, oregano, spices, and flaxseed mixture and pulse again to combine. Transfer to a large mixing bowl, add the cilantro, scallion, and sweet potato, and season generously. Fold to combine, working the sweet potato into the mixture until completely incorporated.

5. Heat the remaining oil in a skillet over medium heat.

6. Take a tablespoon of the mixture and gently form it into a cigarlike cylinder using your fingers. Repeat with the remaining mixture, then add the kofta to the pan in batches and fry for 3 to 4 minutes on each side, or until golden, turning carefully as you go. (Be sure not to overcrowd the pan or the temperature will lower, resulting in the kofta absorbing too much oil.) Transfer to a plate lined with paper towels to drain briefly. Serve hot or cold.

HOT EGGPLANT DIP STEW

SERVES 2

Stews are the backbone of my cooking—they bring solace in times of need and comfort in times of contentment. Here the soft eggplant flesh adds real depth and creaminess to what is a pretty basic chickpea stew, but then again, I've never been ashamed of keeping things simple. The tarragon is a must-have addition, bringing an unusual but moreish aniseedy vibe to the dish and giving it some star quality in the process. Obviously cashew cream solves most ills, but in this instance it plays second fiddle to the eggplant—hot in every sense of the word.

1 large eggplant, halved
2 tablespoons olive oil
1 small red onion, coarsely chopped
2 garlic cloves, minced
2 tarragon sprigs, finely chopped,
    plus extra to garnish
¼ teaspoon cayenne pepper
1 zucchini, halved lengthwise and sliced
2 carrots, halved lengthwise and sliced

1 cup water
1 vegetable bouillon cube
2⅓ cups canned chickpeas, rinsed
    and drained
1 cup Cashew Sour Cream (*see* page 10)
½ cup raisins
sea salt flakes and black pepper
scant 1 cup toasted slivered almonds,
    to garnish

1. Preheat the oven to 425°F.
2. Score the eggplant halves and brush generously with 1 tablespoon of olive oil. Season and place cut-side down on a baking sheet, then bake for 25 to 30 minutes, or until completely soft. Let cool for 5 minutes or so before scooping out the soft flesh and chopping to a fine pulp (don't use the food processor as you want a coarse texture here).
3. Heat the remaining olive oil in a large saucepan over medium heat, add the onion, season, and sweat for 2 to 3 minutes until slightly softened. Add the garlic, tarragon, and cayenne pepper to the pan and sauté for another 3 to 4 minutes, until the onion has softened and is almost translucent.
4. Add the zucchini and carrot to the pan, season, and sauté for 5 minutes, or until softened, then pour over the measured water, add the bouillon cube, and stir to dissolve. Add the chickpeas, bring to a gentle simmer, and cook for 15 to 20 minutes until reduced.
5. Stir in the eggplant pulp and cashew sour cream, season generously with salt and pepper, and simmer for another 10 minutes, adding the raisins right at the end of cooking just to heat through. Divide between plates and sprinkle over the toasted slivered almonds and extra tarragon to garnish. Serve with couscous.

POLENTA "HYGGE" BOWL

with braised bay lentils & harissa-roasted celeriac

SERVES 4

Hygge is a state of mind, in my opinion, but I try to keep my "inner cozy" topped off with wholesome bowls like this one. A vastly underrated ingredient, polenta doesn't naturally have a ton of flavor, which ensures it "perfect backdrop" status, lending its soft yellow hue to more robust accompaniments.

4 cups water

5¼ oz collard greens, sliced

2 teaspoons sea salt flakes

⅔ cup cornmeal

juice of ½ lemon

7 tablespoons plant milk (*see* page 9)

1 tablespoon extra virgin olive oil

2 tablespoons grated vegan parmesan or nutritional yeast (optional)

black pepper

Lentils

1 tablespoon olive oil

1 carrot, grated

3 garlic cloves, minced

1 heaping teaspoon za'atar, plus extra to garnish

½ cup green lentils, rinsed and drained

3 cups water

1 bay leaf

sea salt flakes and black pepper

Celeriac

1 tablespoon harissa paste

2 tablespoons olive oil

juice of ½ lemon

1 celeriac, peeled and cut into cubes

sea salt flakes and black pepper

1. Preheat the oven to 425°F.
2. For the lentils, heat the olive oil in heavy saucepan over medium heat, add the carrot, season, and sauté for 1 to 2 minutes until slightly softened. Add the garlic and za'atar and sauté for another 2 to 3 minutes until aromatic, then stir in the lentils and pour over the measured water. Add the bay leaf, season generously with salt and pepper, and bring to a boil, then reduce the heat to a simmer and cook for around 1 hour, or until the lentils are soft and the sauce has thickened. Keep warm.
3. Meanwhile, make the celeriac. Whisk the harissa, oil, and lemon juice together in a bowl to combine. Arrange the celeriac pieces in a large baking dish, pour over the harissa mixture, and toss to coat, then season and roast for 30 minutes, or until the celeriac is cooked through. Set aside.
4. Bring the measured water to a boil in a saucepan. Add the collard greens to a steamer, set it over the pan, and steam for 2 to 3 minutes, or until wilted. Remove the greens from the steamer and set aside.
5. Add the salt to the water and stir to dissolve, then gradually add the cornmeal, whisking to avoid any lumps. Reduce the heat to low and cook for 15 minutes, stirring frequently, until just beginning to thicken, then stir in the lemon juice, plant milk, olive oil, and parmesan or yeast flakes, if using. Season and cook, stirring, for 1 to 2 minutes more, then remove from the heat and divide among bowls.
6. To serve, spoon the lentils over the polenta, layer over the collard greens and roasted celeriac, and sprinkle over a little extra za'atar to garnish.

TURMERIC & GINGER SWEET POTATO SOUP

with roasted tamari tofu pieces

SERVES 2 TO 4

Fresh turmeric is an obsession of mine. That nubbly little root, boasting a list of medicinal benefits the length of my arm, can basically do no wrong. I pop it in smoothies, oatmeals, and stews—although I especially adore it in soups. Sweet potato and turmeric seems to be the perfect pairing, not least because of their similarly vibrant orange interiors (although that may have something to do with it) but mostly due to the extra, essential "soothe-factor" this root vegetable lends to proceedings. The gorgeous citrus notes of the freshly grated turmeric can't really be replicated by using its more pungent ground cousin but at a pinch a teaspoon of this will still render a pot of pure golden bliss.

1 tablespoon peanut oil

1 onion, finely chopped

2 large sweet potatoes, peeled and coarsely chopped

3 garlic cloves, minced

1 thumb-sized piece of fresh ginger root, peeled and grated

1 thumb-sized piece of turmeric, grated (or 1 scant teaspoon ground turmeric)

1 vegetable bouillon cube

3 cups water, plus extra if necessary

sea salt flakes and black pepper

Roasted tamari tofu

7 oz firm tofu, cut into ¾ inch cubes

2 tablespoons soy sauce or tamari

2 tablespoons peanut oil

½ tablespoon sesame oil

1 tablespoon maple syrup

juice of ½ clementine

To serve

1 to 2 teaspoons dried red pepper flakes

1 tablespoon chopped chives

1. Preheat the oven to 425°F.

2. Heat the peanut oil in a large saucepan over medium heat, add the onion, and sweat for 2 to 3 minutes until it begins to soften.

3. Add the sweet potato to the pan along with the garlic, ginger, and turmeric and cook, stirring, for another 2 to 3 minutes until nicely aromatic. Add the bouillon cube and measured water and stir to dissolve, then bring to a gentle simmer and cook for 20 to 25 minutes, or until the sweet potato pieces are soft.

4. Meanwhile make the tofu. Place the tofu in an ovenproof dish. Whisk the rest of the ingredients together in a small bowl until smooth, pour over the tofu pieces, and toss to combine. Cover with foil and roast for 20 minutes, then remove the foil and roast for another 5 to 10 minutes until golden and glistening. Set aside until needed (the tofu pieces will continue to firm as they cool).

5. Transfer the sweet potato mixture to a blender and blitz until completely smooth, then return to the pan and gently heat through, adding a little extra water if you feel the soup needs thinning out a little.

6. Once heated, divide the soup among bowls and top with the tofu pieces, a sprinkling of red pepper flakes, and some chopped chives.

BAKED APPLE PIE OATMEAL

SERVES 2 TO 4

Apple pie is one of my favorite desserts. This brunch version was a matter of trial and error, before I decided that the vessel in which it is cooked was the most crucial element. Of course, you can sauté the apples in a saucepan and then construct the "pie" in an ovenproof dish, but it doesn't give the same result. Not only does my method save on cleaning the dishes, it also means you can serve the baked oatmeal in slices, thus perpetuating the illusion of a regular pie (albeit one you can enjoy first thing).

1 heaping teaspoon coconut oil

4 sweet eating apples, peeled, cored, and sliced

1 heaping teaspoon ground cinnamon

¼ teaspoon freshly ground nutmeg

3 tablespoons palm sugar

1 tablespoon maple syrup

juice of ½ lemon

pinch of sea salt flakes

1 cup water

2 to 3 tablespoons oat or soy cream, to serve

Oatmeal

1 cup rolled oats

1 teaspoon ground cinnamon

½ teaspoon ground ginger

¼ teaspoon freshly grated nutmeg

¼ teaspoon allspice

pinch of sea salt flakes

7 tablespoons water

⅔ cup almond or other plant milk (*see* page 9)

generous ⅓ cup toasted hazelnuts

⅓ cup golden raisins

1 tablespoon maple syrup

¼ cup slivered almonds

Super-quick maple cream

2 tablespoons light tahini

2 tablespoons maple syrup

pinch of sea salt flakes

1 to 2 tablespoons plant milk (*see* page 9)

1. Preheat the oven to 400°F.
2. For the oatmeal, combine the oats, spices, and salt in a large bowl and pour over the measured water and almond milk. Let soak for 10 minutes.
3. Meanwhile, heat the coconut oil in large ovenproof skillet over medium to high heat. Add the apples and sauté until they begin to soften and color, about 8 to 10 minutes. Sprinkle over the spices and palm sugar and sauté for another 1 to 2 minutes, then add the maple syrup, lemon juice, and salt. Let cook for a few seconds, then pour over the water, increase the heat to high, and let the sauce bubble away for 10 minutes, or until it has begun to thicken and form a loose caramel. Remove from the heat.
4. Add the hazelnuts, golden raisins, and syrup to the oatmeal bowl and stir to combine, then spoon the mixture evenly over the apples in the pan, leaving an outer ring of apple visible. Sprinkle over the slivered almonds and bake for 15 minutes until the apples are bubbling and the oatmeal is golden.
5. Meanwhile, make the maple cream by whisking the tahini, maple syrup, and salt together in a bowl, adding a splash or two of plant milk to give it a pourable consistency.
6. Remove the baked oatmeal from the oven and place it in the middle of the table (where it will take center stage at any casual brunch). Drizzle over the maple and oat creams and serve.

CHOCO CHAI QUINOA BOWL

SERVES 2

I can't decide if this should be a breakfast dish or a dessert. It feels almost too indulgent to be eaten in the morning, but maybe a bit too virtuous to be considered for dessert? You see my quandary. I cook my quinoa before adding it to the chocolate milk mixture, mainly because you don't want the milk to reach boiling point, as it will impair the flavor. The chai spices are the perfect accompaniment to the delicate quinoa, with the fresh cherries offering a welcome nod to summer. For a fun brunch option, fill several small tumblers with the mixture and refrigerate until needed, adding the toppings just before serving. A drizzle of sweetened tahini wouldn't go amiss, either.

¾ cup quinoa (any color)
generous 2 cups water
generous 2 cups unsweetened almond milk
2 tablespoons raw cacao powder or cocoa
1 heaping tablespoon maple syrup
pinch of pink Himalayan salt
1 small cinnamon stick
3 cardamom pods
1 star anise

To serve
handful of cherries, halved and pitted
2 tablespoons toasted coconut flakes
1 oz good-quality semisweet chocolate
   (70% cocoa solids), broken into chunks
½ teaspoon freshly grated nutmeg and/or
   ground cinnamon

1. Add the quinoa to a saucepan and pour over the measured water. Cover with a lid and bring to a boil, then reduce the heat to a simmer and cook for 8 to 10 minutes, or until all the liquid has been absorbed. Remove from the heat and let steam, covered, for 5 minutes, then fluff the quinoa grains up with a fork and set aside (this can be prepared up to a day in advance and kept in a suitable container in the refrigerator until needed).

2. Place the almond milk, cacao, maple syrup, and salt in a saucepan and whisk to combine. Add the spices and bring to a boil, then reduce the heat to low and simmer gently for 10 minutes, whisking occasionally.

3. Taste the hot chocolate milk for sweetness, adding a little extra maple syrup if you feel it needs it, then tumble in the quinoa and heat gently for another 2 to 3 minutes.

4. Divide among bowls and serve topped with cherries, toasted coconut flakes, and a chunk or two of semisweet chocolate, sprinkling over a little freshly grated nutmeg and/or cinnamon to finish.

GET-UP-AND-GO COFFEE SHAKE

SERVES 1 TO 2

A cross between a shake and a smoothie, this morning booster is sure to set you up for the day. I'm crazy about coffee but a pure injection first thing leaves me jittery and even though I'm the furthest thing from a morning person, I prefer not to have a racing heart at 7.30 a.m. I've found that bulking this shake up with banana and oats means I get my caffeine fix without the "climbing the walls" after-effects. If you're really not a coffee drinker, fear not, this tastes just as brilliant without the espresso—pour it in a "to-go" cup and you'll be ready to face the world.

1 banana, sliced and frozen

(1) 1 oz espresso coffee shot

3 medjool dates, pitted

1 tablespoon date syrup

1 heaping tablespoon almond butter

½ cup rolled oats

1 heaping teaspoon maca powder

7 tablespoons plant milk (*see* page 9—oat or almond are my preference)

1. Place everything in a blender and blend until completely smooth. Pour into glasses and serve.

TIP: If you don't have a frozen banana to hand, simply use a regular banana and add a few ice cubes before blending.

NUTS 'N' SEEDS

CHESTNUT & MISO SOUP

with crunchy chickpea croutons

SERVES 2 TO 4

Chestnuts can be found in abundance over the cold winter months and during that time I try to make as much use of them as I can. Because they blend beautifully they make a terrific base for any festive soup, and the result here is a silky-smooth, earthy offering, perfectly set off by the crunchy chickpea croutons. Make this soup in advance and gently heat it through when needed for an easy appetizer to any meal or as an elegant stand-alone lunch dish.

1 tablespoon olive oil
1 red onion, finely chopped
1 carrot, finely chopped
1 garlic clove, minced
7½ oz canned or vacuum-packed chestnuts, crumbled
1½ cups canned chickpeas, rinsed and drained
1 heaping tablespoon miso
generous 2 cups water, plus extra if necessary
sea salt flakes and black pepper

Chickpea croutons
½ cup chickpeas, rinsed and drained
juice of ½ orange
2 tablespoons olive oil
1½ teaspoons maple syrup
2 rosemary sprigs, finely chopped
pink Himalayan or fine sea salt flakes

To serve
soy cream
chopped curly parsley

1. Preheat the oven to 425°F.
2. Heat the olive oil in a saucepan over medium heat. Add the red onion, carrot, and garlic to the pan and sauté for 2 to 3 minutes until starting to soften. Stir in the chestnuts, chickpeas, and miso and cover with the measured water. Bring to a gentle simmer and let cook for 20 minutes.
3. Meanwhile, make the chickpea croutons. Add the chickpeas to an ovenproof dish and whisk the orange juice, oil, and maple syrup together in a bowl to combine. Pour the orange juice mixture over the chickpeas, sprinkle over the chopped rosemary, and generously season with salt. Toss to combine and roast for 25 to 30 minutes, or until golden.
4. Transfer the soup to a blender and blitz until smooth, then return to the pan and heat through, thinning it out with a little extra water, if desired.
5. Ladle the soup into warmed bowls or mugs, drizzle over a little soy cream, and spoon over the crunchy chickpea croutons. Garnish with a sprinkling of chopped parsley and serve.

RED THAI CURRIED POTATOES

with a rich macadamia cream

SERVES 2 TO 4

If I had a spirit vegetable it would be the potato. OK, so the potato is actually interchangeable here, because cauliflower (even sweet potato) would work equally well. The curry paste is just the right side of hot, but the unctuous macadamia cream is truly where it's at. I only use two-thirds of it in the recipe, which may seem a little odd, but I've found that the blender works better when it has more contents to consume. You can keep the remaining cream in the refrigerator for up to 2 to 3 days and stir it through pasta, add it to casseroles, or thin it out to make a sensational salad dressing.

1 heaping teaspoon coconut oil
1 large white onion, sliced
1 lb 2 oz salad potatoes, halved
2½ cups water
1 kaffir lime leaf
sea salt flakes and black pepper
large handful of cilantro leaves,
   to serve

Curry paste
4 red chiles
1 lemon grass stalk
4 garlic cloves
1 thumb-sized piece of fresh ginger root, peeled

4 scallions
juice of 1 lime
½ tablespoon palm sugar
1 heaping teaspoon ground cumin
½ teaspoon ground coriander
2 tablespoons sesame oil
1 teaspoon sea salt flakes

Macadamia cream
¾ cup macadamias, quick-soaked
   and drained (*see* page 8)
⅔ cup filtered water
juice of ½ lime
¼ teaspoon sea salt flakes

1. To make the curry paste, place all the ingredients into a food processor and blend for 1 to 2 minutes until well combined. Set aside until needed.

2. Heat the coconut oil in a heavy saucepan over medium heat. Add the onion, season lightly, and sweat for 5 minutes until translucent.

3. Add the potatoes to the pan, season, and sauté for 2 to 3 minutes, stirring occasionally to prevent sticking, then pour over the curry paste and stir to coat. Cook for 3 to 5 minutes to let the potatoes absorb the flavors in the pan before covering with the measured water.

4. Add the lime leaf to the pan, cover with a lid, and bring to a boil, then remove the lid and reduce the heat to a simmer. Cook, uncovered and stirring occasionally, for 40 minutes, or until the potatoes are completely cooked through.

5. For the macadamia cream, place all the ingredients in a blender and blend vigorously, scraping down the sides from time to time, until completely smooth—this may take up to 10 minutes.

6. Pour two-thirds of the macadamia cream into the sauce and stir to combine, then simmer gently for another 10 minutes. Season to taste and serve garnished with cilantro leaves.

GREEN BEAN SUMMER ROLLS

with a spicy peanut dipping sauce

SERVES 4

Summer rolls are a thing of beauty. Paper thin, they can be filled with just about anything but honestly, it's as if green beans were made to go inside them. They are the perfect length (which saves on chopping), and keeping it an all-green affair just adds to the already uber-fresh vibe of this recipe. Assembling the rolls does take practice and can be time-consuming but when you present a tray of these to guests, their delighted faces will make it all worthwhile.

7 oz green beans, trimmed
1 thumb-sized piece of fresh ginger root, peeled and minced
1 small green chile, minced
1 garlic clove, minced
1 tablespoon soy sauce or tamari
½ tablespoon rice mirin
½ tablespoon lime juice
pinch of pink Himalayan salt
6 Vietnamese rice paper sheets
1 oz salad cress
½ fennel bulb, thinly shaved
1 large scallion, halved and cut into strips
small handful of cilantro, coarsely torn

Peanut dipping sauce
2 heaping tablespoons crunchy peanut butter
1 heaping teaspoon Sriracha or other chili sauce
1 tablespoon soy sauce or tamari
1 tablespoon rice mirin
juice of ½ lime
2 tablespoons water, plus extra if necessary
pinch of sea salt flakes
½ teaspoon black sesame seeds

1. Bring a small saucepan of salted water to a boil. Add the green beans and lightly blanch for 2 to 3 minutes. Drain and rinse under cold water, then transfer to a small mixing bowl.

2. Add the ginger, chile, and garlic to the bowl with the beans and mix together, then add the soy sauce, rice mirin, lime juice, and salt and toss to combine. Set aside until needed.

3. Fill a large mixing bowl with cold water and plunge one of the rice papers into the bowl. Let it soak and soften for up to 1 minute before transferring to a clean dish towel. Carefully reshape the paper so it lies flat before adding your filling.

4. Place a small amount of cress on the half of the soaked paper nearest to you followed by a few green beans and a little fennel, scallion, and cilantro. Using wet fingers, fold the edge farthest from you over the filling and tuck in the sides before carefully rolling the paper away from you to form a neat little wrap. Transfer to a plate and repeat the soaking and filling process until all the ingredients have been used.

5. Place all the dressing ingredients except the sesame seeds into a bowl and whisk to combine, adding a little extra water if the dressing is a bit thick. Pour into a serving bowl and sprinkle over the sesame seeds. Serve with the rolls.

CURRIED CHICKPEA & PINE NUT PASTIES

MAKES 4

If a samosa and a Cornish pasty had a lovechild, it would most probably look a little something like this. A happy marriage of pastry and curried chickpea filling, these mini baked wonders are worth the small amount of effort it takes to make them. The key to pie dough is handling it as little as possible and making sure not to overwork the mixture: pulse until it just comes together and then wrap it tightly in plastic wrap before refrigerating. Avoid the temptation to overfill the pasties, as they may prove difficult to seal. This recipe makes four so if you're serving them at a party (which I heartily recommend) you'll need to double (or maybe even triple) the quantities.

Pie dough
generous ¾ cup gram (chickpea) flour
generous ¼ cup strong white flour
large pinch of sea salt flakes
1 teaspoon garam masala
4 tablespoons olive oil
4 tablespoons water, plus extra if necessary

Filling
3 cups canned chickpeas, rinsed and drained
2 tablespoons pine nuts, toasted
1 scallion, minced
1 garlic clove, minced
1 chile, minced
1 thumb-sized piece of fresh ginger root, peeled and minced
1 tablespoon mild curry powder
juice of ½ lemon
1 heaping teaspoon Dijon mustard
small bunch of cilantro, finely chopped

1. For the pie dough, place the flours, salt, and garam masala in a food processor and pulse to combine. With the engine running, gradually add the oil and the water to form a dough, adding an extra splash or two of water if needed.

2. Turn the dough out onto a clean counter and shape into a ball, then wrap in plastic wrap and transfer to the refrigerator for 20 minutes to rest.

3. Meanwhile, make the filling. Place the chickpeas in a large mixing bowl and coarsely mash. Season generously with salt and pepper, add the rest of the filling ingredients, and mix together thoroughly. Season again to taste and set aside until needed.

4. Preheat the oven to 425°F.

5. Turn the dough out onto a floured counter and divide it into four equal-sized pieces. Shape one of the pieces into a ball, then roll it out into a circular shape to an approximately ¼ inch thickness. Cut the rolled dough circle in half.

6. Take a tablespoon of the filling and place it in one corner of the rolled dough half, leaving enough room around the edges, then fold the dough over the filling and crimp the edges with a fork to seal. Using your hands, shape the samosa into a rough triangular shape, pinching the corners as you go.

7. Place the pasty on a lined baking sheet and repeat the rolling and filling process until all the dough and filling have been used. Bake for 15 minutes until golden and crispy. Serve hot or cold.

GRIDDLED COBB-STYLE SALAD

with a creamy chive dressing

SERVES 2 TO 4

During my time living in Chicago I developed an appreciation for Cobb salad. Blue cheese usually takes center stage, but in this instance (and while there are many convincing vegan alternatives on the market) I've instead enlisted a herby chive dressing, using hummus as the base. I often use hummus in place of cheese—it's particularly wonderful dolloped on pizza and baked. The components of a Cobb salad are typically arranged in neat little rows but because I've opted to griddle the corn and tomatoes, I prefer to place those around the edges, leaving the raw veggies untouched. The real star of the show is the coconut bacon, which is a bit of a revelation—smoked paprika really is a wonder.

½ teaspoon olive oil

4 small corncobs

5¼ oz cherry tomatoes on the vine

1 head of romaine lettuce, coarsely torn or chopped

1 cucumber, halved lengthwise, seeds removed, and sliced

1 ripe avocado, sliced

2 scallions, sliced

large handful of salad cress

Coconut bacon

1¾ cups coconut flakes

2 tablespoons tamari or soy sauce

½ tablespoon balsamic vinegar

½ tablespoon maple syrup

½ teaspoon smoked paprika

Chive dressing

5¼ oz hummus

juice of ½ lemon

¼ teaspoon black pepper

small bunch of chives, chopped

1. Preheat the oven to 400°F and line a baking sheet with parchment paper.

2. To make the coconut bacon, arrange the coconut flakes on the prepared baking sheet in an even layer. Whisk the tamari, balsamic vinegar, maple syrup, and paprika together in a bowl, then pour over the flakes and stir to combine. Bake for 8 to 10 minutes until browned, shaking the pan frequently to prevent burning, then remove from the oven and set aside to cool and firm.

3. Set a large ridged grill pan over medium to high heat and lightly brush with the olive oil. Place the corncobs on the grill pan and cook for 10 to 12 minutes, turning as you go, until charred on all sides, adding the tomatoes to the pan halfway through and turning once until also slightly charred and starting to collapse. Remove the corn and the tomatoes from the pan and let cool slightly.

4. For the dressing, put the hummus, lemon juice, and pepper in a blender and blitz until smooth. Stir through the chives and set aside.

5. Line the bottom of a large platter with the romaine lettuce. Arrange the cucumber slices over the lettuce, place the grilled corncobs and tomatoes around the edges of the platter, and pile the sliced avocado in the center. Drizzle the dressing over the salad and sprinkle over the scallions, coconut bacon, and salad cress. Serve immediately.

SWEET POTATO MASH

with pesto-coated cannellini beans

SERVES 2

I affectionately refer to this dish as my "midweek mania meal," meaning it can be made in a relatively short period of time, is comforting and nourishing in equal measure, and is rather pretty to look at too. Despite it being a three-parter (four if your count the roasted tomatoes), it does feels quite effortless to make. When something tastes this good, who's complaining about a few pots and pans?

1 large sweet potato, peeled and sliced
2 carrots, peeled and sliced
pinch of sea salt flakes
1 teaspoon Dijon mustard
1 to 2 tablespoons extra virgin olive oil
3½ oz cherry tomatoes on the vine
1 tablespoon olive oil
sea salt flakes and black pepper
1 heaping tablespoon chopped basil leaves,
   to garnish

Pesto
1¼ cups basil leaves
1 oz spinach

2 tablespoons toasted walnuts
juice of ½ lemon
1 small garlic clove
5 tablespoons extra virgin olive oil

Beans
½ tablespoon olive oil
1 small white onion, finely chopped
1 garlic clove, finely sliced
2¾ cups canned cannellini beans, drained
   and rinsed
1 cup water
2½ cups coarsely chopped spinach
sea salt flakes and black pepper

1. Preheat oven to 425°F.
2. For the pesto, place all the ingredients in a small food processor and blend to form a coarse paste. Season to taste with salt and pepper and refrigerate until needed.
3. Add the sweet potato, carrot, and salt to a saucepan, cover with water, and bring to a boil. Reduce the heat to a simmer and cook for 15 to 20 minutes, or until soft. Drain and return to the pan, then season to taste, add the mustard and extra virgin olive oil, and coarsely mash. Keep warm on low heat until needed.
4. Place the cherry tomatoes in a baking dish, drizzle over the olive oil, and season. Roast for around 15 minutes until soft and slightly charred, then remove from the oven and set aside until needed.
5. For the beans, heat the olive oil in a skillet over medium heat, add the onion, season with salt, and sweat for 3 to 4 minutes until translucent. Add the garlic to the pan and sauté gently until aromatic, stirring frequently to ensure it doesn't brown. Add the beans, pesto and measured water and heat gently. Add the spinach, cover with a lid, and leave for 2 to 3 minutes, or until wilted. Season to taste.
6. To serve, divide the mash and beans between bowls, top with the roasted cherry tomatoes, and sprinkle over a little chopped basil to garnish.

MASSAGED KALE & TOASTED WALNUT SALAD

with roasted celeriac & persimmon

SERVES 2 TO 4

I fully realize kale has had its moment, but that doesn't mean it isn't still a wondrous little (or rather large) leaf—fibrous, robust, and full of vitamin C. I can't get enough of the stuff and utilize it in just about everything I make, adding it to stews, soups, and even salads. When kale is massaged, its tough exterior eventually yields to reveal a softer side—one that can handle a serious dressing and still hold up to a boatload of toppings too. I've gone down the celeriac path here mainly because it's a perennial fave in our house. I like to call it the "elegant veg" because it has that innate ability to elevate a dish from "hmmm" to "aha!" Persimmon (or Sharon fruit, as it's also known) might seem like an odd inclusion but I simply love fruit in salads and now that persimmons make regular appearances in grocery stores, I thought, Why not?

1 celeriac, peeled and cut into ¾ inch cubes
1 tablespoon canola oil
splash of sesame oil
7 oz curly kale, tough stalks removed and
    leaves torn
1 large persimmon, cut into circles
½ cup toasted walnuts
1 tablespoon chopped chives, to garnish
sea salt flakes and black pepper

Dressing
2 heaping teaspoon whole-grain mustard
juice of ½ orange or 1 clementine
½ tablespoon agave nectar or maple syrup
1 tablespoon soy sauce or tamari

1. Preheat the oven to 425°F.

2. Place the celeriac pieces in an ovenproof dish, pour over the canola and sesame oils, season generously with salt and pepper, and toss to combine. Roast for 40 minutes, shaking the dish from time to time, until tender and lightly golden.

3. Meanwhile, place the kale in a large serving bowl. Whisk the dressing ingredients together and pour over the kale, setting aside a tablespoon or so for serving. Using your hands, massage the dressing into the leaves for 1 to 2 minutes until they begin to wilt and soften. Set aside.

4. Once the celeriac is cooked, remove it from the oven and transfer it to the bowl with the kale. Cut the persimmon circles into quarters and add them to the bowl together with the toasted walnuts. Toss to combine, then drizzle over the remaining dressing and garnish with a few chopped chives. Serve.

CREAMY CURRIED CHICKPEAS

with teriyaki tofu steaks

SERVES 2 TO 4

Midweek meals can often be a struggle. Not wanting to spend an age in the kitchen, we often resort to convenience food or, even worse, a takeout. Thankfully this creamy chickpea curry can be on the table in around 30 minutes, is packed to the rafters with goodness and flavor, and (more importantly) satisfies those postwork comfort-food cravings. For the longest time I associated teriyaki with the bottled sort, without realizing the same result could be achieved in minutes at home. A robust, sticky sauce that will convince even the most hardened tofu-phobes among you, this really is a minor plant-based triumph in bean curd form. I beg you to put your fears aside and give these "steaks" a whirl before writing this much-maligned ingredient out of your life completely. I have a funny feeling you won't regret it.

½ tablespoon coconut oil

1 red onion, finely chopped

1 thumb-sized piece of fresh ginger root,
    peeled and minced

2 garlic cloves, minced

1 green chile, minced

1¾ cups canned chickpeas, rinsed and
    drained

1 teaspoon ground turmeric

1 heaping teaspoon garam masala

¼ teaspoon chili powder

1 heaping teaspoon tomato paste

1 to 2 tablespoons water

1¼ cups canned coconut milk

1 kaffir lime leaf

½ tablespoon palm sugar

1 heaping teaspoon cornstarch

handful of kale

⅓ cup golden raisins

sea salt flakes and black pepper

1 tablespoon finely chopped mint, to garnish

cooked basmati rice, to serve

Teriyaki tofu

7 tablespoons water

scant ¼ cup tamari

scant ¼ cup rice mirin

1 thumb-sized piece of fresh ginger root,
    peeled and minced

1 garlic clove, minced

2 tablespoons agave nectar

1 teaspoon tomato paste

juice of ½ lemon

(1) 14 oz firm tofu block, pressed (*see* page 11)
    and cut into 4 equal-sized wedges

½ teaspoon olive oil

1. Heat the coconut oil in a large saucepan over medium heat. Add the onion, season, and sweat for 4 to 5 minutes until translucent. Add the ginger, garlic, and chile to the pan and cook, stirring, for another 2 to 3 minutes until aromatic.

2. Tumble in the chickpeas and sprinkle over the turmeric, garam masala, and chili powder. Stir to coat, season generously, and cook for 2 to 3 minutes until the spices are nicely toasted. Stir through the tomato paste and loosen with a splash of water, then pour over the coconut milk, add the lime leaf, and

palm sugar and season generously. Bring to a simmer, cover with a lid, and let simmer for
15 minutes.

3. Meanwhile, for the teriyaki tofu, place all the ingredients, except the tofu and oil, into a saucepan and bring to a boil, then reduce to a simmer and cook for 5 to 10 minutes, or until thickened and reduced. Take off the heat and let cool slightly.

4. Place the tofu wedges in a baking dish. Pour over two-thirds of the teriyaki sauce and brush to coat.

5. Dissolve the cornstarch in a little water and whisk into the curry sauce. Add the kale and raisins and simmer for another 10 to 15 minutes.

6. Set a ridged grill pan over medium to high heat and lightly brush with the oil. Add the tofu wedges and griddle for 10 to 12 minutes, turning, until marked on all sides. Remove from the heat and brush over the remaining teriyaki sauce while they are still warm.

7. Spoon the curry into warmed bowls, top with the tofu steaks, and garnish with some finely chopped mint. Serve with basmati rice.

CRISPY POTATO FRIES

with a parsley & almond sauce

SERVES 4

I'm as big a French fries fan as the next person but even I need to shake it up now and again. Sliced into circles and roasted in olive oil, these feel almost like a slightly more voluptuous chip—although with enough fluffy potato to make them worth your while. Once the potatoes are roasted and golden, up the ante with this parsley and almond sauce. I prefer to keep things on the rustic side, which lends itself rather well to scooping. In my world, these fries and a few cold beers is usually just what the physician ordered.

12 oz baking potatoes, cut into ½ inch circles
1 tablespoon olive oil
1 teaspoon dried red pepper flakes
1 teaspoon garlic powder
sea salt flakes and black pepper

Sauce
**large bunch of flat-leaf parsley, leaves and
    stalks**
scant ⅔ cup slivered almonds
1 sprig rosemary
1 shallot
1 garlic clove
1 tablespoon cider vinegar
juice of ½ lemon
7 tablespoons extra virgin olive oil
5 tablespoons water, plus extra if necessary

1. Preheat the oven to 425°F. Line a baking sheet with parchment paper.

2. Arrange the potato circles on the prepared sheet in an even layer, drizzle over the olive oil, and sprinkle over the red pepper flakes and garlic powder. Season with salt and pepper and roast for 35 to 40 minutes, or until golden and crispy.

3. Meanwhile, make the sauce. Place all the ingredients in a blender or food processor and pulse to combine, then blend briefly to a coarse pestolike consistency, adding a little more water if necessary.

4. Transfer the fries to a large platter and spoon the parsley sauce over the top. Serve at once.

COCONUT-CRUSTED POTATOES

SERVES 2 TO 4

On the face of it this is a rather strange (and mildly off-putting) combo. My inner Irish girl is shouting "no!" while my 21st-century vegan taste buds are saying, "by golly, this actually works." The dry unsweetened coconut really does transform into the most delicious coating without any notion of sweetness, giving the humble roast potato a nifty makeover that would make any dinner guest happy. I often serve these alongside my Celeriac Steaks (*see* page 166) and a decent helping of delicate pea shoots. In a way, this recipe is a weird nod to the queen of glamorous dining, the incomparable Nigella Lawson. Although heaven knows what she'd make of a coconut-encrusted potato.

> 1¾ lb salad potatoes
> scant ½ cup dry unsweetened coconut
> 3 tablespoons coconut oil
> sea salt flakes

1. Preheat the oven to 475°F.

2. Peel the potatoes and halve the slightly larger ones to ensure they are all evenly sized, then place them in a saucepan and season generously with sea salt. Cover with water and bring to a boil, then reduce the heat to a simmer and cook for 10 minutes, or until just starting to cook through.

3. Drain and return the potatoes to the pan. Shake it vigorously to roughen up the edges slightly (this will help the potatoes crispen up in the oven), then add the dry unsweetened coconut and toss to coat.

4. Add the coconut oil to a baking sheet, transfer to the oven, and leave for 4 to 5 minutes, or until melted and nice and hot. Tumble in the potatoes and toss to coat in the oil (if it's hot enough, they should sizzle and splutter immediately), then roast for 40 minutes until golden and crispy, shaking the pan from time to time.

5. Once cooked, season generously with sea salt and serve.

RED PESTO RISOTTO

with shaved asparagus

SERVES 4

Risotto is the most restorative dish I can think of, and I know that getting a pot of it on the go will soon put my worries at ease. Halfway between a romesco sauce and a regular pesto, this simple red sauce is something special, whether you stir it through risotto, use it as a dip or dollop it over roasted veg. I urge you to keep a batch to hand (it will keep for up to 1 week in the refrigerator). You won't regret it.

7 oz asparagus spears, trimmed	Pesto
1 vegetable bouillon cube	¾ cup blanched almonds
1½ tablespoons olive oil	6 sundried tomatoes
1 onion, finely chopped	1¼ cups basil
1 celery stalk, finely chopped	½ cup cherry tomatoes
1 garlic clove, minced	1 garlic clove, minced
1 cup arborio rice	grated zest and juice of 1 lemon
juice of ½ lemon	7 tablespoons extra virgin olive oil
sea salt flakes and black pepper	sea salt flakes and black pepper

1. To make the pesto, place the almonds in a food processor and pulse until they form a coarse meal. Add the sundried tomatoes, basil, cherry tomatoes, garlic, lemon zest and juice, and half the olive oil and season generously. Blend again, drizzling in the remaining oil until it forms a coarse paste. Transfer to a container and refrigerate until needed.

2. Bring 6⅓ cups water to a boil in a saucepan, add the asparagus, and blanch for 2 to 3 minutes, then remove with a slotted spoon and refresh immediately under cold water. Set aside.

3. Add the bouillon cube to the pan, stir to dissolve, and reduce the heat to a very gentle simmer.

4. Heat 1 tablespoon of the olive oil in a heavy saucepan over medium heat. Add the onion and celery, season, and sweat for 5 minutes until translucent. Add the garlic and sauté for 1 to 2 minutes until aromatic, then add the rice and stir to coat.

5. Add the hot broth to the pan a few ladlefuls at a time until the rice is covered. Bring to a simmer and cook over medium heat, stirring frequently, until most of the liquid has been absorbed. Continue to cook, stirring and ladling in the broth a little at a time, until the rice is just cooked.

6. Meanwhile, shave the blanched asparagus with a vegetable peeler or slice lengthwise into thin strips. Heat the remaining olive oil in a small grill or ridged grill pan over medium–high heat, add the asparagus strips, season, and stir-fry for 1 to 2 minutes until lightly charred or golden. Squeeze over the lemon juice and remove from the heat.

7. Remove the risotto from the heat and stir through 3 heaping tablespoons of the pesto along with a splash more broth to loosen everything up.

8. Divide the risotto among bowls, topping each with an additional spoonful of the pesto and several strips of the stir-fried asparagus.

DILL-COATED CASHEW CHEESE

with homemade "nut-pulp" crackers

SERVES 4 TO 6

The one stumbling block that most people encounter when first embarking on or even considering a vegan lifestyle is cheese. I therefore offer up a plant-based solution that might just ease the way. Without getting involved with full-on fermenting, this is the most straightforward vegan cheese you're likely to come across. Investing in a nut-milk bag or cheesecloth is essential here, because that is what will help make our "cheese" as firm as possible. Using this as a base you can add just about anything you like—think of this recipe as a blank canvas and get creative.

Being the thrifty person I am, I cannot contemplate throwing anything away—not even the dregs of nut milk. These crackers were a happy accident, the result of a bid to use up a mountain of the stuff I'd accumulated after a mammoth plant-milk making session (yes, my life really is that exciting). I pretty much always have a batch stored in an airtight jar, ready to be dipped in hummus or to be spread with the above-mentioned creamy "cheese." Even my die-hard omnivore friends are obsessed.

1⅔ cups cashews, soaked and drained
    (*see page 8*)
1 tablespoon coconut oil
grated zest and juice of ½ lemon
1 teaspoon cider vinegar
1 garlic clove (or ¼ teaspoon garlic granules)
2 teaspoons fine sea salt flakes
pinch of white pepper
2 heaping tablespoons nutritional yeast
    (optional)
1 heaping tablespoon finely chopped dill
dried or fresh fruit, to serve

"Nut-pulp" crackers
1 tablespoon milled flaxseed
1½ cups reserved nut milk pulp (*see page 9*)
    or ground almonds
scant ½ cup spelt flour
½ teaspoon sea salt flakes
⅓ cup pumpkin seeds
⅓ cup sunflower seeds
1 tablespoon chia seeds
1 tablespoon coconut oil
1 tablespoon agave nectar or maple syrup
5 heaping tablespoons sesame seeds

1. Add the cashews to a food processor and blitz until reasonably smooth. Add the coconut oil, lemon juice, cider vinegar, garlic, salt, pepper, and nutritional yeast, if using, and blitz until completely smooth, scraping down the sides from time to time.

2. Check seasoning, then transfer to a large piece of cheesecloth or a nut-milk bag and wrap tightly into a ball. Suspend over a bowl and chill for at least 2 to 3 hours, or overnight for a firmer texture.

3. Unwrap the cheese ball and use your hands to shape it into your desired form—I like a slightly domed ball.

4. Lightly mix the dill and lemon zest in a bowl, add the cheese, and roll to coat evenly. Cover with parchment paper, wrap in plastic wrap, and refrigerate until needed.

5. To make the nut-pulp crackers, preheat the oven to 340°F. Mix the flaxseed with 3 tablespoons of water and set aside.

6. Place the nut-milk pulp, spelt flour, salt, and the pumpkin, sunflower, and chia seeds in a large mixing bowl and mix together with your hands to combine.

7. Melt the coconut oil in a small pan over low heat and whisk in the agave nectar and 7 tablespoons water. Add to the nut pulp mixture along with the flaxseed solution and incorporate using a spatula.

8. Tip the mixture onto a large piece of parchment paper and flatten slightly. Place another piece of parchment paper on top and roll or press into as thin a square as possible without it breaking—a thickness of about 1/16 inch. Carefully remove the top layer of parchment paper, trim the edges of the dough, and prick all over with a fork.

9. Transfer to a baking sheet, sprinkle over the sesame seeds, and bake for 25 to 30 minutes, or until completely dry but not overcooked. Remove from the oven and let cool completely before breaking into shards. Serve alongside the cashew cheese and a selection of dried and/or fresh fruit such as sliced pear or apple.

"GOES-WITH-EVERYTHING" TAHINI SAUCE

MAKES APPROX. 7 TABLESPOONS

If ever there was a go-to sauce in my kitchen this is it. Whenever I put a batch on the table at dinner parties or gatherings it is devoured with alarming gusto, usually amid questions of "but what is it?" I like it reasonably runny but you can add more or less water to suit—it's worth the effort to get the consistency just right, as the sauce is not going to have the same luscious effect if it's too stiff.

3 heaping tablespoons tahini

juice of ½ lemon

¼ teaspoon sea salt flakes

½ tablespoon cider vinegar

½ tablespoon maple syrup

3½ to 5 tablespoons water

1. Place the tahini in a bowl, add the lemon juice, salt, vinegar, and maple syrup and whisk to combine. Gradually add the water until you achieve your desired consistency (you may not need all of it).

VARIATIONS

> Swap out the lemon for any citrus fruit you fancy—it works particularly well with orange.

> For a more pungent sauce, add some minced garlic.

> For a more fragrant sauce, stir through some chopped fresh herbs.

> For a richer sauce, swap the cider vinegar for balsamic—a splash of pomegranate molasses also works well in this scenario.

> For a sweet sauce, remove the lemon, cider vinegar, and salt and replace with the juice of ½ orange. Increase the sweetener content to 2 tablespoons and whisk vigorously together with 3½ tablespoons water until smooth, then drizzle over freshly baked Pumpkin Muffins (*see* page 235).

SAVORY FIG & WALNUT STUFFING SLICE

SERVES 8 TO 10

I'm often asked what I eat at Christmas or for Sunday lunch and for the last four-plus years the answer has been something along the lines of this. Similar to a traditional stuffing (although with a bit more to it), this is a reliable recipe that is sure to satisfy. If you can, leave the pan with the mixture in it in the refrigerator overnight before baking—this will result in a firmer texture and make it much easier to cut. While this stuffing slice is terrific with potatoes, gravy, and all the trimmings, I look forward to eating it cold in sandwiches, slathered in mustard, and served with a few dill pickles. Heaven.

7 oz stale whole-wheat bread

1 cup toasted walnuts

4 tablespoons olive oil

2 celery stalks, finely diced

3 shallots, finely diced

3 garlic cloves, minced

1 lb 2 oz parsnips, grated

5¼ oz carrots, grated

1 heaping teaspoon dried oregano

2 heaping teaspoons whole-grain mustard

3 tablespoons dairy-free margarine

6 dried figs, finely chopped

small bunch of flat-leaf parsley, finely
    chopped

sea salt flakes and black pepper

1. Place the bread in a food processor and pulse to form fine bread crumbs. Season generously, add the toasted walnuts, and pulse again to combine. Set aside until needed.

2. Heat 1 tablespoon of the olive oil in a large pan over medium heat. Add the celery, shallots, and garlic to the pan, season, and sweat for 4 to 5 minutes until translucent.

3. Add the parsnip, carrot, and oregano to the pan, season generously, and sauté for 5 minutes until softened. Reduce the heat to low, add the whole-grain mustard, margarine, remaining olive oil, and the bread crumb mixture and stir well to combine, then remove the pan from the heat and stir through the chopped figs and parsley.

4. Spoon the stuffing mixture into a lightly greased 1 lb loaf pan a little at a time, pressing down firmly with the back of a spoon to compact it nicely. Cover with aluminum foil and refrigerate overnight (you can cook it straight away but this chilling will result in a firmer slice).

5. When ready to cook, preheat the oven to 425°F.

6. Bake covered for 45 minutes, then remove the foil and bake for another 10 to 15 minutes until nicely browned. Remove from the oven and let cool in the pan for at least 10 minutes before gently tipping it out onto a serving plate. Cut into slices and serve.

WASABI-ROASTED SPROUTS

SERVES 4

Holler if you love sprouts! Once much maligned, these leafy beauties have officially been given a 21st-century makeover thanks to our current obsession with all things green. As for baby corn—what is this precisely? It always reminds me of that scene from *Big* when Tom Hanks nibbles around the edges of a tiny cob and is left with a limp little stalk. Halved and roasted, however, is definitely where it's at when it comes to these bad boys. Spruced up with a dash of wasabi? Now you're talking.

14 oz Brussels sprouts, halved lengthwise
5¼ oz baby corn, halved lengthwise

Marinade
1 heaping teaspoon wasabi powder
juice of ½ orange
1 tablespoon soy sauce or tamari
2 tablespoons sesame oil (cold-pressed if possible)
½ tablespoon rice mirin
½ tablespoon maple syrup

To serve
1 heaping tablespoon chopped cilantro
1 scallion, sliced
1 tablespoon sesame seeds
zest of 1 orange
2 to 3 tablespoons "Goes-with-Everything" Tahini Sauce (*see* page 151)

1. Preheat the oven to 425°F.
2. Place the sprouts and baby corn in an ovenproof dish.
3. To make the marinade, put all the ingredients in a small bowl and whisk together to combine.
4. Pour the marinade over the veg, toss to combine, and bake for 25 to 30 minutes, giving the pan a little shake from time to time, until tender and lightly golden.
5. Remove the veg from the oven and transfer to a serving dish. Scatter over the cilantro, scallion, sesame seeds, and orange zest, and finish with a generous drizzle of "goes-with-everything" tahini sauce, if desired.

FRAGRANT FRIED RICE

with toasted almonds & raisins

SERVES 2 TO 4

If you're seeking a midweek stunner that takes very little prep, this stir-fried rice recipe is just the ticket. I've lost count of the many variations on this super-simple supper I've made over the years, but I always come back to this almond and raisin combo. Crunch and chew are essential components of any vegan dish, in my opinion, and this humble bowl is no exception. This fried rice also makes for a tremendous side dish or you can serve it as part of everyone's current favorite go-to meal, the Buddha bowl. Load it up with tofu and kale and you've got yourself a winner. Fuss-free dining at its best.

generous 1 cup brown or white basmati rice

½ lemon

1 star anise

1 small cinnamon stick

3 cardamom pods

5 cloves

generous 1½ cups water

1 tablespoon coconut oil

1 small onion, sliced

1 large carrot, sliced

1 celery stalk, sliced

2 tablespoons tamari or soy sauce, plus extra
    to serve

1 thumb-sized piece of fresh ginger root,
    peeled and minced

1 large garlic clove, minced

1 green chile, seeds removed and minced

1 tablespoon rice wine or cider vinegar

1 heaping tablespoon chopped mint

1 heaping tablespoon chopped tarragon

⅓ cup golden raisins

scant ⅔ cup toasted slivered almonds

1. Rinse the rice thoroughly and place in a saucepan with the lemon, star anise, cinnamon, cardamom, and cloves. Pour over the measured water, cover with a lid, and bring to a boil, then reduce the heat to a simmer and cook for 10 minutes, or until most of the liquid has been absorbed. Remove from the heat and set aside to steam, covered, for 5 minutes before removing the lemon and spices and fluffing up the rice grains with a fork.

2. Heat the coconut oil in a large skillet or wok over medium to high heat. Add the onion, carrot, and celery and sauté for 4 to 5 minutes until they begin to soften. Pour over half the tamari, stir in the ginger, garlic, and chile, and sauté for another 3 to 5 minutes until nicely aromatic.

3. Add the rice to the pan and stir to combine, then pour over the rice wine vinegar and remaining tamari and sauté for another 5 minutes, or until the rice is heated through and starts to catch slightly on the bottom of the pan.

4. Add the chopped herbs, raisins, and almonds to the pan, setting aside a little of each for garnish. Stir to combine before spooning onto a large platter or into individual serving bowls. Garnish with the reserved herbs, raisins, and toasted slivered almonds and serve with extra tamari for drizzling.

STIR-FRIED BROCCOLI

with toasted peanuts

SERVES 2 TO 4

I'm a side-dish fanatic and broccoli is my jam. Don't try to substitute the sprouting variety suggested here with the thicker, more treelike type, as their long fibrous stems are an integral part of the recipe. And avoid overcooking the broccoli at all costs—you want it just soft but far from floppy. The roasted peanuts bring crucial crunch; I tend to coarsely chop them but you could pulverize them using a mortar and pestle, if desired. You can also try cashews for a similar result.

½ cup peanuts
1 tablespoon sesame oil
7 oz sprouting broccoli
1 to 2 tablespoons water
1 tablespoon rice mirin
3 tablespoons soy sauce or tamari
½ tablespoon maple syrup
2 scallions, finely sliced

1. Preheat the oven to 425°F.
2. Arrange the peanuts on a baking sheet and toast in the oven for 10 to 15 minutes until golden, shaking the pan from time. If the peanuts have skins, transfer them to a clean dish towel and rub them vigorously to remove. Coarsely chop and set aside until needed.
3. Heat the sesame oil in a large skillet over medium to high heat. Add the broccoli and stir-fry for 3 to 4 minutes until just beginning to color. Add the measured water, cover with a lid, and let steam for 2 to 3 minutes, or until the broccoli has softened.
4. Remove the lid, add the rice mirin, soy sauce, and maple syrup to the pan, and stir-fry for 2 to 3 minutes, or until the liquid has reduced to a glossy sauce.
5. Add the sliced scallion and toasted peanuts and cook, tossing to combine, for another 1 to 2 minutes. Serve.

BAKED POTATO NACHOS

with saucy black beans & avocado crema

SERVES 2 TO 4

This is my kind of food. Easy to assemble but packed to the rafters with flavor, it's a veritable smorgasbord for the senses. The halved potatoes take virtually no time to cook and require minimal input—for what might look like a long list of ingredients, you'll be amazed at how easily this whole dish comes together.

2 small baking potatoes, halved and scored
2 small sweet potatoes, halved
1 tablespoon olive oil
sea salt flakes and black pepper

Avocado crema
1 ripe avocado
⅔ cup coconut or soy yogurt
juice of ½ lemon
1 garlic clove, minced
sea salt flakes

To serve
1 scallion, sliced
1 x Quick-Pickled Red Onions (*see* page 184)
small handful of cilantro leaves, torn

Black beans
1 tablespoon olive oil
1 small red onion, finely chopped
3 garlic cloves, minced
1 teaspoon dried oregano
1 teaspoon ground cumin
½ teaspoon ground coriander
¼ teaspoon cinnamon
1 teaspoon dried red pepper flakes
2¼ cups canned black beans in their liquid
1 tablespoon balsamic vinegar
sea salt flakes and black pepper

1. Preheat the oven to 425°F. Line a baking sheet with parchment paper.
2. Brush the potato and sweet potato halves with the oil, season with salt and pepper, and bake for 30 to 40 minutes, or until cooked through.
3. Meanwhile, make the black beans. Heat the olive oil in a large skillet over medium heat. Add the onion to the pan, season, and sweat for 4 to 5 minutes until translucent. Add the garlic and oregano and sauté for 1 to 2 minutes until aromatic, then add the spices and fry gently for several seconds before adding the black beans in their liquid. Season generously with salt and pepper, stir in the balsamic vinegar, and simmer for 20 minutes until the sauce has thickened and reduced. Mash the beans lightly, leaving some beans whole, remove from the heat, and set aside.
4. For the avocado crema, mash the avocado and transfer to a bowl along with the yogurt, lemon juice, and garlic. Season with salt and stir to combine.
5. Remove the potatoes from the oven and arrange on a large platter. Spoon over the black beans, top with the avocado crema, and garnish with the scallion, pickled red onion, and cilantro leaves. Serve.

EARTHY

QUINOA & CANNELLINI BEAN SOUP

SERVES 4

The inspiration for this dish came via the Internet, specifically a travel diary of sorts on YouTube. The video followed a fabulously hippy vegan's exploits in Peru. In a snippet of no more than 5 seconds in length, she was served a bowl of soup in a magnificently ramshackle establishment of the kind that you just know serves the best food. All I could think was that I'd be willing to fly halfway around the world to sample that exact bowl of plant-based awesomeness, but then reality kicked in and I realized I'd have to make do with creating my own. I watched that same "blink and you'll miss it" shot on repeat, until I was satisfied I'd got the gist of the dish. Of course, I can't be sure about the seasonings used, but by golly if this is not the most comforting bowl of goodness ever to pass my lips. And in deference to the place that inspired it and the hippy who led me to it, I vow to make that voyage to Peru one day.

1 tablespoon canola oil

1 large scallion, chopped

1 celery stalk, chopped

1 green bell pepper, cored, seeded, and diced

1 small green chile, minced

3 garlic cloves, finely sliced

small bunch of cilantro, leaves stripped and stalks minced

10½ oz salad potatoes, cut into ½ inch circles

generous ½ cup quinoa (any color), rinsed

4 cups water

1 vegetable bouillon cube

1½ cups canned cannellini beans, rinsed and drained

sea salt flakes and black pepper

1¾ oz lightly salted tortilla chips, to garnish

1. Heat the canola oil in a heavy saucepan over medium heat. Add the scallion, celery, and pepper, season, and sweat for 2 to 3 minutes until starting to soften.

2. Add the chile, garlic, and cilantro stalks to the pan and sauté gently until aromatic, about 2 to 3 minutes. Add the potato and quinoa to the pan and stir to combine, then pour over the measured water and bouillon cube and stir to dissolve. Bring to a gentle simmer, cover with a lid, and cook for around 30 minutes, or until the potato and quinoa are completely cooked.

3. Add the cannellini beans to the pan, season, and cook for another 5 to 10 minutes, or until the beans are warmed through. Divide the soup among heated bowls and garnish with the cilantro leaves and a few lightly salted tortilla chips.

GARLICKY PAN-FRIED MUSHROOMS

SERVES 2

Simple food is where my heart truly lies. Minimizing ingredients and effort while maximizing flavor has become something of an obsession. These garlicky mixed mushrooms are an ideal brunch or quick lunch idea (and are particularly wonderful when served with my favorite Easy Wheaten Loaf, *see* page 224) and can be whipped up in mere minutes—my kind of cooking. For an extra fancy touch, stir through some tangy cashew sour cream or even a dollop of yogurt, as well as a handful of quickly wilted spinach or arugula. This is what I call no fuss, no drama, just easy plant-based food.

1 tablespoon coconut oil
1 large shallot, sliced
1 rosemary or thyme sprig, leaves stripped and coarsely chopped
14 oz mixed mushrooms, trimmed and coarsely torn
juice of ½ lemon

3 garlic cloves, minced
3½ oz spinach
3 tablespoons Cashew Sour Cream (*see* page 10)
sea salt flakes and black pepper
freshly toasted Wheaten Bread (*see* page 224), to serve

1. Heat the coconut oil in a large skillet over medium heat. Add the shallot, season, and sweat for 2 to 3 minutes until translucent.

2. Stir in the chopped rosemary and cook for 1 to 2 minutes, then add the mushrooms and a squeeze of lemon juice. Increase the heat to medium to high and sauté for 5 to 7 minutes until the mushrooms begin to color and reduce.

3. Add the garlic and remaining lemon juice to the pan and cook, stirring, for 3 to 4 minutes, or until nicely aromatic. Add the spinach and cook, stirring, until gently wilted, then stir through the cashew sour cream.

4. Check for seasoning and serve on top of freshly toasted wheaten bread.

TLT SOURDOUGH SANDWICH

SERVES 2

Tofu bacon is having a bit of a moment and rightly so. Tofu (and tempeh) lends itself brilliantly to this intoxicatingly pungent marinade, with the result being far from anything you'd expect from "bland" bean curd. It continues to firm up when cooling, so don't be tempted to overbake it even if it initially feels a little soft to the touch. I normally set it aside for a few minutes before serving, although quite honestly I prefer it cold—it is a snack in itself (extras can be kept in an airtight container in the refrigerator for up to 1 week), and I have used it in everything from salads to sushi. It might just be my new favorite thing.

2 tablespoons egg-free mayo
4 sourdough bread slices
2 teaspoons Dijon mustard
1 Boston lettuce, leaves separated
1 beefsteak tomato, sliced
sea salt flakes and black pepper
2 dill pickles, to serve

Tofu bacon
(1) 12 oz firm tofu or tempeh block, pressed (*see* page 11)
1 tablespoon tomato paste
2 tablespoons soy sauce or tamari
1 tablespoon balsamic vinegar
1 teaspoon smoked paprika
1 tablespoon maple syrup
½ tablespoon blackstrap molasses
1 tablespoon melted coconut oil (or other vegetable oil)
1 to 2 tablespoons water

1. Preheat the oven to 425°F.
2. For the tofu bacon, cut the tofu block into ¼ inch slices (or slightly thicker if using tempeh). Place the rest of the bacon ingredients in a shallow bowl and vigorously whisk to combine, then dip each tofu slice into the marinade to coat evenly. Transfer to a baking sheet and bake for 25 to 30 minutes, turning halfway through cooking, until nicely browned and fim. Remove from the oven and leave for 5 minutes to cool and firm further.
3. Spread a little mayo over one slice of sourdough bread and a little Dijon mustard over another. Layer the lettuce and tomato over one of the slices and season with salt and pepper, then top with a few slices of the tofu bacon and a final, generous smear of mayo before sandwiching the slices together. Cut diagonally and serve with a few dill pickles.

CELERIAC STEAKS

with a mushroom stroganoff sauce

SERVES 4

Celeriac steaks are something of a stunner. Not only do they slice beautifully but they also cook in no time, meaning that dinner can be on the table in 30 minutes. The creamy stroganoff sauce is a simple but beautiful accompaniment, and could easily be served alongside rice for a bowl-food type scenario if desired. For me though, the star of the show is the roasted celeriac, which has solved many a weeknight dinner dilemma in our house, as well as becoming a bit of a last-minute dinner party staple.

1 large celeriac, peeled and cut into 4 slices, each 1 inch thick
1 tablespoon olive oil
sea salt flakes and black pepper
1 heaping tablespoon chopped chives, to garnish

Stroganoff sauce
1 tablespoon olive oil
1 leek, trimmed, cleaned, and finely chopped
1 lb 2 oz cremini mushrooms, trimmed and sliced
2 garlic cloves, minced
grated zest and juice of 1 lemon
pinch of cayenne pepper
1 cup soy, oat, or other plant cream
1 teaspoon Dijon mustard
sea salt flakes and black pepper

1. Preheat the oven to 475°F. Line a baking sheet with parchment paper.

2. Brush the celeriac slices with the olive oil, season generously, and place on the prepared sheet. Roast for 20 minutes, then turn and cook for another 10 to 15 minutes, or until nicely browned around the edges. Remove from the oven and set aside.

3. For the stroganoff sauce, heat the olive oil in a large skillet over medium heat. Add the leek, season, and sweat for 2 to 3 minutes until softened.

4. Add the mushrooms to the pan, season generously, and stir to combine. Cook for 5 minutes, without stirring, until just beginning to color, then add the garlic, lemon zest, cayenne pepper, and 1 tablespoon of the lemon juice. Season with salt and pepper and cook for another 5 to 10 minutes until the mushrooms have shrunk and are lightly golden.

5. Pour over the soy cream, stir in the Dijon and remaining lemon juice, and bring to a gentle simmer. Cook, stirring, for 1 to 2 minutes, thinning out the sauce with a splash of water if it becomes too thick. Season to taste.

6. Divide the celeriac steaks among plates and top each with a spoonful or two of the stroganoff sauce. Garnish with a sprinkling of chopped chives and serve with a fresh pea shoot salad.

EASY FLATBREADS FROM SCRATCH

MAKES 6 TO 8 FLATBREADS

Flatbreads are a super lunchtime option. The dough itself requires very little attention and the toppings are as flexible as you please. I'm hooked on this red bell pepper and white bean duo but mashed avocado works just as well. I also like to serve these sandwiches at casual gatherings, simply arrange them on a large plate or platter and let everyone help themselves. Alternatively, you could lay out a selection of different toppings and let them create their own—interactive dining at its best.

scant 1⅔ cups spelt flour
½ teaspoon instant yeast
½ teaspoon baking powder
¼ teaspoon sea salt flakes
1 tablespoon poppy seeds
scant 1 cup warm water
½ tablespoon agave nectar or maple syrup
1½ tablespoons coconut oil, melted
2 heaping tablespoons pumpkin seeds

Smoky sautéed bell pepper strips
1 heaping teaspoon coconut oil
1 large red bell pepper, cored, seeded, and sliced
1 teaspoon smoked paprika
½ teaspoon za'atar
sea salt flakes and black pepper

Easy white bean spread
2 cups canned cannellini beans, rinsed and drained
1 tablespoon tahini
1 garlic clove, minced
grated zest and juice of ½ lemon
small bunch of cilantro
3 tablespoons extra virgin olive oil

1. In a large mixing bowl, combine the spelt flour, yeast, baking powder, salt, and poppy seeds.

2. In a separate bowl, whisk together the measured water, agave nectar, and 1 tablespoon of the coconut oil to combine. Make a well in the center of the flour and pour over the liquid, using a fork to gradually work the flour into the liquid in a clockwise motion until it forms a sticky dough.

3. Tip the dough onto a clean, floured counter and knead for up to 10 minutes, adding a little more flour if necessary, until smooth and elastic. Rub the dough in the remaining melted coconut oil, return to the mixing bowl, cover with a clean dish towel, and set aside for 10 minutes to rest.

4. Meanwhile, prepare the red bell pepper. Heat the coconut oil in a skillet over medium heat. Add the bell pepper and season lightly, then sprinkle over the smoked paprika and za'atar and sauté for 5 minutes until softened. Set aside until needed.

5. For the white bean spread, place all the ingredients in a food processor and blend until smooth.

6. Wipe the skillet clean, turn the heat up to high, and heat until smoking. Divide the dough into 6 to 8 equal size pieces and shape and roll each into rough, circular pizza-style pitas. Add the breads to the pan one at a time and cook for 3 to 4 minutes until they begin to puff up, then flip and cook for another 1 to 2 minutes until puffed and lightly charred.

7. Spread the flatbreads with the white bean spread, layer over the smoky sautéed bell pepper strips, and sprinkle over the pumpkin seeds to finish.

BELUGA LENTIL & BLACK OLIVE DIP

SERVES 4

Dips are an essential part of most cooks' repertoires and while I probably lean on hummus (the original and best) a little too much, I do occasionally venture outside my comfort zone. I adore the rustic brown hue of this lentil offering and even more so the earthy olive overtones that make it a perfect pairing for a slice of fresh crusty white bread and a glass of red wine. Heaven. Almost akin to a paté, this dip would make an excellent appetizer divided into smaller pots or you could serve it up in one large shallow bowl as part of a casual gathering, finished with a slick of good-quality olive oil and a smattering of pickled peppercorns and my perennial favorite, capers. If you're also stuck in a bit of a hummus rut, may I suggest a trip down lentil lane?

1¼ cups precooked beluga lentils
generous ¾ cup cashews, soaked and drained
   (see page 8)
1 garlic clove, minced
2 heaping tablespoons chopped black olives
juice of ½ lemon
1 to 2 tablespoons water
scant ¼ cup extra-virgin olive oil
sea salt flakes and black pepper

To serve
1 tablespoon chopped black olives
1 teaspoon baby capers
½ teaspoon pickled peppercorns, coarsely
   chopped
1 tablespoon extra virgin olive oil

1. Place the lentils, cashews, garlic, olives, lemon juice, and water in a food processor. Season generously and blend together, gradually drizzling in the olive oil as you go, until the mixture is thick and smooth with no lumps remaining.

2. Season to taste. Serve immediately, or refrigerate until needed—the dip will keep for up to 3 to 4 days in an airtight container—garnishing with a few finely chopped black olives, a smattering of capers, some pickled peppercorns, and a generous drizzle of extra virgin olive oil.

RUSTIC LEEK, POTATO & ARTICHOKE GALETTE

SERVES 4 TO 6

Galettes are essentially fuss-free pies that actually benefit from looking a little rough around the edges. The tattier the better when it comes to encasing whatever filling you choose—I've opted for classic potato and leek, as well as some precooked artichokes for good measure. This rustic delight makes for a sensational centerpiece and I often serve it as part of a Sunday lunch. It's so satisfying no one will be leaving the table hungry … and if you do happen to have leftovers, it's particularly good eaten cold too.

2 large potatoes, quartered
1 heaping teaspoon coconut oil
3 leeks, trimmed, cleaned, halved
    lengthwise, and sliced
3½ oz artichokes in oil, sliced
1 to 2 teaspoons olive oil
sea salt flakes and black pepper
large handful of dill, chopped, to garnish

Pie dough
scant 1⅓ cups all-purpose or spelt flour
7 tablespoons dairy-free margarine or
    vegetable shortening
pinch of fine sea salt flakes
¼ teaspoon brown sugar
2 to 3 tablespoons ice-cold water

1. Preheat the oven to 475°F.
2. For the pie dough, place the flour, margarine, salt, and sugar in a large mixing bowl or food processor and lightly rub or pulse together to form a bread crumblike mixture. Add the water a tablespoon at a time and work or pulse together to form a dough (being careful not to overwork it at this point). Roll the dough into a ball, wrap it tightly in plastic wrap, and refrigerate for up to 30 minutes.
3. Meanwhile, add the potatoes to the pan, cover with water, and season generously with salt. Bring to a boil, then reduce the heat, and simmer gently for 15 to 20 minutes, or until cooked through. Drain and let cool, then cut into ½ inch slices and season.
4. Heat the coconut oil in a small skillet over medium heat, add the leeks, and sweat lightly for 3 to 4 minutes until softened. Season and set aside.
5. Remove the dough from the refrigerator and roll it out on a lightly floured counter to a ¼ inch thickness.
6. Transfer the rolled dough to a lightly floured baking sheet and arrange the leeks in the center, leaving a 2 to 2¾ inch border around the edges. Layer over the potato slices and artichokes and drizzle over a little olive oil. Gently fold the dough inward to secure the filling and bake for 30 minutes, turning the sheet halfway through to ensure an even bake.
7. Remove from the oven and let cool slightly, then slice and sprinkle over a little chopped dill to garnish. Serve.

PAN-FRIED RED CABBAGE

with a herby tofu mayo

SERVES 4

I can't say silken tofu is a mainstay in my kitchen but that doesn't mean it doesn't have its uses. The herby tofu mayo is one such triumph that is so unnervingly like the real thing, it even has me second-guessing. Served alongside the pan-fried cabbage, it's a seriously rich side dish that really packs a punch on the both the texture and flavor front. I like to keep the red cabbage on the crunchier side but if you prefer it slightly more tender, then clamp on a lid during the cooking time to let it steam and soften. Don't scrimp on the mayo however—the bigger the dollop the better.

1 tablespoon olive oil	Herby tofu mayo
1 small red cabbage, coarsely chopped	**10½ oz silken tofu**
1 garlic clove, finely sliced	**1 heaping teaspoon coconut oil, melted**
grated zest and juice of 1 lemon	**juice of ½ lemon**
5 to 6 radishes, sliced	**1 garlic clove, minced**
2 tablespoons toasted pumpkin seeds	**1 teaspoon Dijon mustard**
sea salt flakes and black pepper	**1 teaspoon agave nectar or maple syrup**
	¼ teaspoon sea salt flakes
	1 heaping tablespoon chopped chives

1. To make the herby mayo, place the tofu, coconut oil, lemon juice, garlic, Dijon mustard, agave nectar, and salt in a blender and blend until completely smooth. Season to taste, then transfer to a bowl, stir through the chives, and refrigerate until needed.

2. Heat the olive oil in a large skillet over medium to high heat. Add the cabbage and garlic to the pan, season generously, and stir-fry for 10 to 12 minutes, or until it begins to soften.

3. Squeeze over the lemon juice and stir through the sliced radish, then remove from the heat and transfer to a serving bowl. Sprinkle over the lemon zest and pumpkin seeds and dollop over the mayo to finish.

FALAFEL-STUFFED MUSHROOMS

with kale & quinoa tabbouleh & a coconut & mint dressing

SERVES 4

I'm always searching for ways to make falafel more interesting. Using it as a stuffing made so much sense and I wasn't disappointed with the result. However, it's the pistachio dust accompaniment that is perhaps the more exciting revelation. I sprinkle it over everything from pasta to avocado toast.

3 cups canned chickpeas, rinsed and drained, setting aside 1 tablespoon of liquid
scant 1½ cups flat-leaf parsley
2 garlic cloves
1 scallion
1 small green chile
2 tablespoons lemon juice
4 portobello mushrooms, trimmed and stalks removed
2 to 3 tablespoons olive oil
1 teaspoon ground cumin
½ teaspoon ground coriander
sea salt flakes and black pepper

Kale & quinoa tabbouleh
1 tablespoon olive oil
1 leek, trimmed, cleaned, halved lengthwise, and sliced
1 cup quinoa, rinsed
1 bay leaf
grated zest and juice of ½ lemon
3½ oz kale, tough stalks removed and leaves coarsely chopped
scant 2¼ cups flat-leaf parsley
1 tablespoon extra virgin olive oil
pinch of sea salt flakes
pinch of black pepper

Pistachio "dust"
⅓ cup pistachios
2 teaspoons nutritional yeast
pinch of sea salt flakes

Coconut & mint dressing
3 tablespoons coconut yogurt
1 tablespoon tahini
juice of ½ lemon
pinch of sea salt flakes
1 heaping tablespoon finely chopped mint

1. Preheat the oven to 400°F.
2. To make the pistachio "dust," place the pistachios, nutritional yeast, and salt together in a food processor and pulse together until the mixture resembles dust. Set aside until needed.
3. For the coconut and mint dressing, put the coconut yogurt, tahini, lemon juice, and salt in a bowl and mix together until smooth, then stir through the mint. Refrigerate until needed.
4. Put the rinsed chickpeas in a clean dish towel and rub them until the skin comes off (this is optional but it does result in a better falafel mixture). Place the chickpeas, parsley, garlic, scallion, chile, lemon juice, and reserved chickpea liquid in a food processor and pulse until it forms a coarse but spreadable paste. Season with salt to taste.
5. Brush the mushrooms all over with the oil. Season the insides with a little salt and pepper and sprinkle over the ground cumin and coriander. Divide the chickpea mixture between the mushrooms

equally and top each with a generous sprinkling of pistachio dust. Bake for 45 minutes until tender and lightly golden.

6. To make the tabbouleh, heat the olive oil in a large skillet over medium heat. Add the leek, season, and sweat for 2 to 3 minutes until it begins to soften, then add the quinoa, bay leaf, and lemon zest. Pour over generous 2 cups water, cover, and bring to a boil, then reduce the heat to a gentle simmer and cook for around 10 to 12 minutes, or until all the water has been absorbed. Remove from the heat.

7. Add the kale to the pan, then cover and leave for 2 to 3 minutes, or until the kale is gently wilted. Stir through the parsley, lemon juice, olive oil, salt, and pepper.

8. To serve, spoon the warm quinoa tabbouleh onto plates and top with the stuffed mushrooms, adding a dollop of the coconut dressing on the side and a sprinkling of the pistachio "dust" to finish.

INDIVIDUAL MUSHROOM WELLINGTONS

SERVES 4

Ready-made pastry to the rescue, this time in the form of mushroom Wellingtons—sensational centerpieces for any meal. The trick is to tuck the pastry tightly around the mushroom, making sure there are no air bubbles, so that it shrinks as the mushrooms cooks and reduces. Serve with steamed green beans and a few simply boiled salad potatoes for an elegant supper.

2 tablespoons olive oil	1½ teaspoons yeast extract
3 shallots, finely chopped	4 large portobello mushrooms, trimmed
4 large garlic cloves, minced	3½ oz kale, leaves torn and stems removed
1¼ cups green lentils, rinsed and drained	juice of ½ lemon
2 bay leaves	2 sheets of vegan ready-made puff pastry,
3 cups water	thawed if frozen
1 vegetable bouillon cube	sea salt flakes and black pepper

1. Heat 1 tablespoon of the olive oil in a large saucepan over medium heat. Add the shallots to the pan, season, and sweat for 2 to 3 minutes until translucent. Stir in the garlic and sauté for 1 to 2 minutes, then add the lentils, bay leaves, measured water, and bouillon cube. Stir to dissolve the bouillon cube, bring to a gentle simmer, and cook for 40 minutes, or until most of the liquid has been absorbed and the lentils are tender and almost cooked through.

2. Stir the yeast extract through the lentils and simmer for another 5 to 10 minutes, or until all the liquid has been absorbed. Remove from the heat and let cool, then spoon the mixture over the mushrooms. Set aside.

3. Heat the remaining olive oil in a skillet over medium heat. Add the torn kale, season generously, and heat, stirring occasionally, until gently wilted. Squeeze over the lemon juice and let cool.

4. Preheat the oven to 425°F.

5. Roll the pastry sheets out on a floured counter slightly to enlarge each by about a third, then use a saucer as to template to cut out 8 pastry circles. Cut simple leaf-shape decorations out of the excess pastry.

6. Place a small heap of kale in the center of 4 of the pastry circles and lay over the mushrooms, lentil-stuffed side down. Place the remaining pastry circles on top (rolling them out a little more first if you need to for fit) and pinch the sides together with a fork. Trim off any excess pastry and tuck in any gaps as you go, ensuring there are no air bubbles around the mushrooms.

7. Gently press 2 pastry "leaves" onto each Wellington and bake for 30 to 35 minutes until golden and crispy. Remove from the oven and let cool slightly before serving.

HERBY LENTIL & SAVOY CABBAGE COBBLER

with savory oaty scones

SERVES 4

Anything that has been topped with mashed potato and then baked is heaven, but I think there's an even more satisfying option out there—the savory oaty scone. The less you handle the scone mixture the better to ensure a light, crumbly texture. I think savoy cabbage is such an underused vegetable but in this rather lovely stew it really comes into its own, bringing with it a wonderful texture.

1 tablespoon olive oil

1 leek, trimmed, cleaned, and sliced

3 garlic cloves, minced

1¼ cups Puy lentils, rinsed and drained

1 vegetable bouillon cube

1 bay leaf

1 small butternut squash, peeled and chopped

1 tablespoon tomato paste

½ savoy cabbage, roughly sliced

⅓ cup soy cream

sea salt flakes and black pepper

1 tablespoon chopped chives, to garnish

Scones

1 teaspoon cider vinegar

7 tablespoons soy milk

1½ cups rolled oats

1 heaping teaspoon marjoram

¼ teaspoon fine sea salt flakes

½ tablespoon sugar

1 teaspoon baking powder

½ teaspoon baking soda

3½ tablespoons dairy-free margarine

1. Heat the olive oil in a large saucepan over medium heat. Add the leek, season, and sweat for 2 to 3 minutes until it begins to soften, then add the garlic and cook for another 1 to 2 minutes, or until nicely aromatic.

2. Add the lentils, bouillon cube, bay leaf, and 3 cups water, bring to a simmer, and cook for 10 to 15 minutes until the lentils have softened and the sauce has reduced slightly, then stir in the butternut squash and tomato paste. Cover and simmer for another 20 minutes, or until the squash is cooked through.

3. Add the cabbage and cook, covered, for 5 to 10 minutes, or until wilted. Pour over the soy cream, season, and simmer gently for 2 to 3 minutes, then remove from the heat and set aside until needed.

4. Preheat the oven to 475°F.

5. For the scones, combine the cider vinegar and soy milk in a bowl and set aside for 5 to 10 minutes to let the mixture curdle.

6. Place the oats in a blender and blend together to form a fine flour, then transfer to a large mixing bowl. Add the marjoram, salt, sugar, baking powder, and baking soda and whisk to combine, then work the margarine into the flour using your fingertips until the mixture resembles bread crumbs. Make a well in the center and pour over the curdled soy milk mixture, then stir together gently with a metal spoon to form a loose, wet dough.

7. Turn the scone dough out onto a lightly dusted counter and shape it into a rough ball, then use a dusted rolling pin to roll it out to about a ¾ inch thickness. Cut the biscuits out using a 2½ inch pastry

cutter. Roll the excess into a rough ball and repeat until all or most of the dough is used—you should get about 8 scones from the mixture. Lightly dust the tops with flour.

8. Transfer the stew to a large ovenproof dish and top it with the scones. Bake for 15 minutes, or until the scones have risen slightly and are perfectly crumbly. Sprinkle over the chopped chives and serve.

ROASTED RED ONION & BUTTERNUT SQUASH SALAD

with black quinoa

SERVES 2 TO 4

Warm salads are always welcome in my kitchen. Assembling such dishes is the best part of making them, of course, ensuring that everything is shown off to its perfectly roasted best. The black quinoa can obviously be substituted with the regular (or red) kind but I do have a penchant for the extreme nuttiness of this variety. The sunflower seed dressing is surprisingly cheesy—a quality I sometimes play with by adding a handful of chopped chives before blending.

2 red onions, cut into wedges

1 butternut squash, cut into wedges

1 heaping teaspoon ground cumin

1 teaspoon sumac

1 teaspoon sea salt flakes

1 tablespoon balsamic vinegar

1½ teaspoons pomegranate molasses

2 tablespoons olive oil

1 cup black quinoa, rinsed and drained

generous 2 cups water

5¼ oz savoy cabbage, sliced

juice of ½ lemon

3 dried figs, chopped

black pepper

Sunflower seed dressing

½ cup sunflower seeds, plus extra to garnish

1 small garlic clove, minced

juice of ½ lemon

¼ teaspoon sea salt flakes

⅔ cup water

1. Preheat the oven to 425°F.

2. Arrange the onion and butternut squash wedges in a large baking dish, sprinkle over the cumin, sumac, and salt and toss to combine. Drizzle over the balsamic vinegar, pomegranate molasses, and 1 tablespoon of the olive oil and roast for 35 to 40 minutes, shaking the pan from time to time, until cooked through and golden.

3. Meanwhile, place the quinoa and measured water in a saucepan, cover with a lid, and bring to a boil, then reduce the heat to a simmer and cook for 10 to 15 minutes until the water is completely absorbed. Remove from the heat and set aside to steam, covered, for 2 to 3 minutes.

4. Heat the remaining 1 tablespoon of olive oil in a skillet over medium heat. Add the cabbage, season, and gently sauté until it begins to wilt, then add the quinoa and stir to combine. Squeeze over the lemon juice, season generously, and stir through the chopped figs. Remove from the heat and set aside until needed.

5. To make the dressing, place all the ingredients in a blender and blitz until completely smooth, scraping down the sides from time to time as you go.

6. Transfer the quinoa to a large platter and distribute the red onion and butternut squash over the top. Drizzle over the dressing and sprinkle over extra sunflower seeds to garnish.

SWEET POTATO STUFFED SHELLS

SERVES 2 TO 4

If you're after pure unadulterated comfort food then look no further than these stuffed pasta shells. Filled with an incredibly easy sweet potato mixture that mimics all the greatness of a regular mac and cheese, this is a dish I return to so frequently it's become something of a personal classic. I like to retain a little texture by avoiding mashing the sweet potatoes to oblivion—and, perhaps more importantly, ensuring the shells are cooked al dente so as not to turn to mush in the oven. Err on the side of caution and drain the pasta several minutes before the cooking time recommended on the package for a perfect piping hot pasta bake with the ultimate plant-based twist.

1 tablespoon olive oil

2 leeks, trimmed, cleaned, and finely chopped

1 lb 2 oz sweet potatoes, peeled, halved, and thinly sliced

3 cups boiling water

1 vegetable bouillon cube

⅔ cup soy, oat, or coconut cream

juice of ½ lemon

10½ oz conchiglioni (large pasta shells)

1 heaping tablespoon nutritional yeast or vegan parmesan-style cheese

sea salt flakes and black pepper

To serve

1 heaping tablespoon chopped chives

1 tablespoon extra virgin olive oil

1. Preheat the oven to 400°F.

2. Heat the olive oil in a large shallow skillet over low heat. Add the leek, season, and sweat for 2 to 3 minutes, or until it begins to soften. Add the sweet potato slices, season, and cook, stirring occasionally, for 1 to 2 minutes, then pour over the boiling water. Add the bouillon cube and stir to dissolve, then bring to a simmer and cook for 15 minutes, or until the sweet potato is soft.

3. Mash the sweet potato in the pan with a fork or potato masher to form a thick, creamy sauce (it should still have some texture to it, so don't worry if it's not completely smooth). Let simmer for another 10 to 15 minutes, until slightly thickened and reduced, stirring in the soy cream and squeezing over the lemon juice in the last few minutes of cooking. Season to taste, cover with a lid, and remove from the heat.

4. Bring a large saucepan of salted water to a boil, add the pasta shells, and cook for 12 to 15 minutes until not quite al dente, or for just slightly under the recommended cooking time. Drain and let cool slightly.

5. Cover the bottom of a baking dish with a layer of the sweet potato sauce. Carefully stuff the pasta shells with the remaining sauce and arrange neatly in the dish, then sprinkle over the nutritional yeast or vegan parmesan and bake for 15 to 20 minutes until bubbling and golden.

6. Remove from the oven and let cool slightly before serving, sprinkling over some finely chopped chives and a good glug of extra virgin olive oil to finish.

STEAMED BUNS

with shredded hoisin mushrooms & quick-pickled red onions

SERVES 4

There are some dishes I set aside for very special occasions—ones where I know a little impressing is required. And even though there's not a huge amount of effort involved in these steamed buns (enough but not insurmountable), they still retain that air of being a treat. Because they're so innately tactile, they make gatherings go with a bang. The dough can be made ahead of time, wrapped in plastic wrap, and refrigerated. Unless you happen to have an impressive collection of steaming baskets, you'll probably need to steam them in several batches, although in my opinion the expectation is half the fun.

¾ cup lukewarm water
1½ teaspoons instant yeast
1 tablespoon olive oil
1 tablespoon sesame oil
scant 2½ cups all-purpose flour
¼ teaspoon baking soda
¼ teaspoon sea salt flakes
2 tablespoons light brown sugar
small handful of cilantro, chopped, to garnish

Sprouts
7 oz Brussels sprouts, shredded
pinch of pink Himalayan salt
juice of ½ lemon
½ tablespoon rice mirin

Quick-pickled red onions
1 red onion, finely sliced
1 teaspoon sea salt flakes
1 teaspoon light brown sugar
1 tablespoon rice mirin
1 tablespoon cider vinegar
1 teaspoon black sesame seeds

Shredded hoisin mushrooms
1 tablespoon olive oil
14 oz cremini mushrooms, trimmed and
    shredded into thin strips
1 tablespoon soy sauce
½ tablespoon rice mirin
4 tablespoons hoisin sauce
1 tablespoon lemon juice

1. Whisk the measured water and yeast together in a large mixing bowl until frothy. Add the oils and whisk again. Gently combine the flour, baking soda, salt, and sugar and gradually add to bowl. Mix until it forms a rough dough ball, folding in a little at time. Tip the dough out onto a lightly floured counter and knead for up to 10 minutes, or until the dough is smooth and elastic. Place in a lightly oiled mixing bowl, cover with a dish towel, and set aside to rise for 2 hours.
2. For the pickled onions, place the onion in a bowl, cover with boiling water, and set aside to soak for 30 minutes. Drain and return to the bowl, then add the salt, sugar, rice mirin, and cider vinegar. Stir to coat and set aside to pickle until needed.
3. Put the sprouts in a bowl, sprinkle over the salt, squeeze over the lemon juice and rice mirin, and toss to combine. Set aside until needed.
4. For the hoisin mushrooms, heat the olive oil in a skillet over medium heat, add the mushrooms, and cook, stirring occasionally, until colored. Add the soy sauce and rice mirin, increase the heat to

medium to high, and sauté for 1 to 2 minutes, then add the hoisin and lemon juice and cook for another 1 to 2 minutes. Remove from the heat, cover with a lid, and set aside until needed.

5. Set a steamer basket over a saucepan one-third full of simmering water.

6. Punch the air out of the risen dough and knead it again for a few seconds, then shape the dough into a ball and divide it into 16 equal-sized pieces. Roll each piece into a ball and then out into a disk, then brush one side of the disks with sesame oil and fold over. Place the folded buns on a small piece of parchment paper and transfer them to the steamer, being careful not to overcrowd the basket (you may need to do this in batches). Steam for 6 to 7 minutes.

7. Sprinkle the black sesame seeds over the pickled red onion.

8. To serve, fill the steamed buns with a spoonful of the hoisin mushrooms and top with the red onion and sprouts. Garnish with some cilantro and devour.

SWEETLY DOES IT

HASSELBACK APPLES

with a coconut caramel sauce

SERVES 6 TO 8

These apples are too cute for words. If you're after an impressive dessert that is seriously simple to make, this is it. Yes, it's just an apple, but it's a perfectly soft and sweet one. Truthfully the wow factor is all down to the caramel sauce, which is something of a game changer. I must admit that prior to this I was something of a palm-sugar-phobe, as I felt it was a bit of a con—sugar is sugar, and all that. However, after experimenting with various different sugars in a bid to bring you the ultimate vegan caramel (it's a tough job), I'm a total convert. Don't panic if you can't get your hands on any though, the caramel works equally well with soft brown sugar, although it won't quite have that depth of flavor the palm variety brings to the table. I now keep a batch of this sauce in my refrigerator at all times and slather it on everything from toast to ice cream … and it's also pretty wonderful straight off the spoon.

4 large apples, peeled, cored, and halved
¼ teaspoon freshly grated nutmeg
½ teaspoon ground cinnamon
½ tablespoon coconut oil, plus extra
    for brushing
1 tablespoon maple syrup
⅓ cup toasted walnuts, crushed

Coconut caramel sauce
½ cup coconut palm sugar
½ cup water
½ cup canned coconut milk (or cream)
1 teaspoon vanilla extract
pinch of sea salt flakes

1. Preheat the oven to 400°F and brush the bottom of a large ovenproof dish with a little coconut oil.

2. For the sauce, place the coconut palm sugar and water in a saucepan, bring to a boil, and cook for 5 to 7 minutes, swilling the pan to move the contents around but not stirring, until the mixture has reduced and the palm sugar has completely dissolved. Whisk in the coconut milk and simmer vigorously for 7 to 10 minutes until thick and glossy, then remove from the heat and whisk in the vanilla extract and salt. Transfer to a suitable container and refrigerate until needed.

3. Place the apple halves flat-side down on a counter and use a sharp knife to make thin cuts (do not cut the apples all the way through).

4. Place the apples flat-side down in the prepared dish and dust with the nutmeg and cinnamon. Melt the coconut oil and maple syrup together in a small saucepan before brushing over the apples, then loosely cover with foil and bake for 20 minutes until cooked through.

5. Remove the apples from the oven and carefully transfer to individual serving dishes or a large sharing platter. Drizzle over the caramel sauce and sprinkle over the crushed walnuts before serving.

"DOLE WHIP" NICE CREAM

SERVES 4

Unless you're a die-hard Disney fan like me you're probably wondering what on earth "Dole Whip" is. Let me tell you, you are in for a treat. On a baking hot day, having traipsed through just about every land the Magic Kingdom has to offer, you will find yourself at a stall selling what I can only describe as heaven in a plastic cup. If you like soft-serve ice cream and have a penchant for pineapple then this, my friends, is exactly what you've been waiting for. Made using fresh pineapple, unlike the Disney version (although that too is 100 percent vegan!), this dairy-free delight is precisely what the physician ordered, whether you're sweating it out in Florida or sitting in your backyard. Bliss, I tell you. Bliss.

> **1 small pineapple, peeled and cut into coarse chunks**
> **2 ripe bananas, peeled and cut into coarse chunks**
> **grated zest and juice of 1 lime**
> **3 tablespoons maple syrup or agave nectar**

1. Put the pineapple and banana chunks into zip-lock bags, transfer to the freezer, and freeze overnight.

2. The next day, place the frozen pineapple and banana chunks in a food processor along with the rest of the ingredients. Pulse to break the ingredients down before blending for 2 to 3 minutes, stopping and scraping down the sides from time to time, until the mixture resembles soft-whip ice cream (it will go through several stages to get to this point, so be patient). Spoon into tall glasses and serve immedately.

MATCHA & LIME PIE

with macerated strawberries

SERVES 8 TO 10

The vibrant green hue of this (nearly) no-bake dessert coupled with the insane red of the macerated strawberries is precisely why I love to wheel this dish out at dinner parties—after all, we do eat with our eyes. The agar agar flakes ensure a firm pie that slices beautifully. If you are unfamiliar with this handy little ingredient, you'll soon get the hang of using it. The trick is to allow the flakes to dissolve in water without stirring (although occasional swirling is encouraged) before pouring the liquid into the cashew/tofu mix. You'll end up with a wonderfully zesty filling with an uplifting hint of matcha, which helpfully boosts both flavor and color too—double whammy. Your friends and family are bound to be impressed.

Crust
¾ cup dry unsweetened coconut
generous ¾ cup pistachios
generous ¾ cup Brazil nuts
1⅓ cups dried apricots
¼ teaspoon vanilla powder or ½ vanilla bean, split and seeds scraped
pinch of sea salt flakes
1 tablespoon coconut oil

Filling
1⅓ cups cashews, soaked overnight and drained (*see page 8*)

5¼ oz silken tofu
grated zest and juice of 6 limes
scant ½ cup agave nectar or maple syrup
1 heaping tablespoon matcha powder
pinch of sea salt flakes
1 cup water
2 tablespoons agar agar flakes

Macerated strawberries
2 cups strawberries, hulled and sliced
juice of 1 lime
½ vanilla bean, seeds scraped
3 tablespoons palm sugar

1. Preheat the oven to 400°F.
2. To make the crust, place the dry unsweetened coconut, pistachios, and Brazil nuts in a blender or food processor and pulse together to form a fine crumblike texture. Add the apricots, vanilla powder, salt, and coconut oil and blend for 1 minute, or until it just comes together (pinch some of the mixture between your fingers to test—if it sticks easily, you're good to go).
3. Transfer the crust mixture to a 9 inch fluted tart pan and press into the bottom and sides to cover evenly. Bake for 8 to 10 minutes, or until lightly colored, then remove from the oven and let cool in the refrigerator until needed.
4. For the filling, add the cashews to a blender together with the tofu, lime zest and juice, agave nectar, matcha powder, and salt. Blend for 10 to 15 minutes, or until the mixture is completely smooth. (If it is not entirely silky, keep blending until you achieve the desired consistency, otherwise it will negatively affect the texture.)
5. Meanwhile, place the water in a small saucepan and sprinkle over the agar agar. Do not stir. Bring

to a boil, then simmer over medium heat for 5 to 10 minutes, or until the agar agar has dissolved and the water has reduced by about a third.

6. Add the agar agar liquid to the blender with the pie filling and blend until it is completely incorporated, scraping down the sides from time to time, then pour the filling over the cooled crust, smoothing the top with the back of a spatula. Cover with plastic wrap and refrigerate for 4 to 6 hours, or until set.

7. For the macerated strawberries, put the berries, lime juice, vanilla seeds, and palm sugar into a bowl, stir to combine, and refrigerate for at least 30 minutes, or until needed, bringing the berries to room temperature before serving.

8. Pile the strawberries over the center of the pie to serve.

WATERMELON WEDGE PARTY CAKE

SERVES 8 TO 10

Party food doesn't necessarily have to be unhealthy. While sugar-laden cakes are a welcome occasional treat, sometimes I like to serve something that is both equal amounts virtuous and yummy. There is no conceivable way your guests will be disappointed with this quirky little fruit cake, especially once you cut into it and reveal its uber-pink interior—cue the "wows." The toasted coconut gives it some wonderful crunch, while the lightly whipped coconut cream exudes "excuse me while I lick the bowl" factor in abundance. A terrific option for a kids' party (especially if they've already loaded up on candies and whatnot), this cake is an easy way to bring things down a notch in the chaos department without them feeling like they're being cheated. Win-win.

1 small seedless watermelon
9 oz carton coconut cream, chilled
grated zest and juice of ½ lime
3 tablespoons agave nectar
1 cup toasted coconut flakes
4 to 5 strawberries, halved, to decorate

1. Slice both ends off the watermelon and place it cut-end down on a cutting board. Using a sharp knife, cut away the remaining rind to create a loose cakelike shape, trimming the sides to square things up a little. Transfer to a serving plate.

2. Place the chilled coconut cream in a stand mixer, add the lime zest and juice and agave nectar, and beat on high speed until thick, fluffy, and cloudlike (alternatively, put everything in a bowl and beat together use a handheld electric whisk). Refrigerate for 10 minutes to chill and firm.

3. Once chilled, dollop the whipped coconut cream on top of the watermelon and ease it down the sides with a spatula to coat—don't worry if it slides off to begin with, just work it up the sides until it adheres. Sprinkle over the toasted coconut and decorate with fresh strawberries. Time to party!

COCONUT & CARDAMOM MACAROONS

with a simple chocolate coating

MAKES 12 MACAROONS

These easy macaroons were created with my mom in mind. Since going plant-based, they are the one treat she really misses, as unfortunately most store-bought varieties contain egg. The cardamom is a classic inclusion, which is complemented by the touch of lemon (although lime would also be lovely). But what's particularly great about these macaroons is that they can be either baked or chilled to equally yummy effect. Quite honestly I can't decide which version I prefer. Dipped and drizzled in chocolate—the darker the better—they've fast become one of my favorite sweet treats, and thankfully my mom likes them too. You can shape the mixture into bars, rather than mounds, if you prefer.

8 cardamom pods

2⅔ cups dry unsweetened coconut

grated zest of 1 lemon

½ cup agave nectar or other vegan sweetener

1 vanilla bean, split lengthwise and seeds
  scraped

3 tablespoons coconut cream

1 heaping tablespoon coconut oil

⅓ cup crushed pistachios

Coating

2 tablespoons coconut oil

3 tablespoons raw cacao powder

1 tablespoon rose water

2 tablespoons agave or maple syrup

pinch of pink Himalayan salt

1. If baking the macaroons, preheat the oven to 400°F and line a baking sheet with parchment paper.
2. Remove the seeds from the cardamom pods and grind to a fine powder in a mortar and pestle.
3. Place the ground cardamom in a food processor along with the dry unsweetened coconut, coconut cream, lemon zest, agave nectar, vanilla seeds, and coconut oil. Pulse until the mixture comes together. To test, pinch a small amount between your fingers—if it adheres easily it's ready to shape.
4. Take a tablespoon of the coconut mixture, shape it into a mound, and place it on the prepared baking sheet. Repeat with the rest of the mixture, then bake the macaroons for 10 to 12 minutes until golden before setting aside to cool, or simply refrigerate them for 30 minutes until firm.
5. To make the coating, melt the coconut oil in a small saucepan over low to medium heat. Remove from the heat and add the cacao powder, rose water, agave syrup and salt. Gently stir until the mixture thickens and becomes smooth and glossy. If the mixture appears grainy, return to the pan to a low heat and stir for a few seconds until the texture changes.
6. Dip the bottom of each macaroon in the cacao mixture to coat, then transfer to a baking sheet to cool. Once all the macaroons have been dipped, drizzle the remaining coating over the tops and sprinkle over the pistachios. Let the chocolate coating set slightly, then return to the refrigerator for 30 minutes, or until the chocolate coating has hardened completely. Enjoy straight away or keep in an airtight container in the refrigerator for up to 1 week.

DAIRY-FREE HAZELNUT & CHOCOLATE SPREAD

MAKES APPROX. 5½ OZ

Nut butters are easier to make than you'd imagine—all it takes is a little patience with the food processor. This spread is as wonderful on toast as it is dolloped in oatmeal or even straight from the jar.

scant 1¼ cups hazelnuts
1 heaping tablespoon raw cacao powder
3 tablespoons maple syrup

7 tablespoons almond or soy milk
¼ teaspoon ground cinnamon
pinch of sea salt flakes

1. Preheat the oven to 425°F.

2. Place the hazelnuts on a baking sheet, transfer to the oven, and toast for 5 to 7 minutes, shaking the baking sheet from time to time, until lightly golden.

3. Remove the nuts from the oven and let cool before placing them in a clean dish towel and rubbing them vigorously to remove the skins. Transfer to a food processor and pulse to form a coarse crumblike consistency.

4. Add the cacao, maple syrup, plant milk, cinnamon, and salt to the processor and blend together until the mixture forms a smooth, spreadable paste—loosening the mixture with a little extra plant milk if necessary. Transfer to a clean jar and keep refrigerated for up to 14 days.

BRAZIL-NUT CHAI STEAMER

SERVES 2

When I was at drama school in London, we would often have a morale-saving "steamer" at the coffee shop in King's Cross Station. This is my homage to those ice-cold days, being told we'd never make it …

5 cardamom pods
generous ¾ cup Brazil nuts
½ cinnamon stick
¼ teaspoon vanilla powder
3 tablespoons agave nectar

¼ teaspoon black pepper
pinch of sea salt flakes
1 star anise
5 to 6 cloves
¼ teaspoon ground cinnamon, to serve

1. Remove the cardamom seeds from their pods and grind to a fine powder with a mortar and pestle.

2. Place the ground cardamom, Brazil nuts, cinnamon stick, vanilla powder, agave nectar, black pepper, salt, and 2½ cups filtered water in a blender and blend until smooth.

3. Strain the mixture through a nut-milk bag, cheesecloth, or strainer, then transfer the milk to a saucepan and add the star anise and cloves. Heat gently over very low heat, stirring continuously, until the mixture is steaming—being sure not to let it boil or simmer.

4. Pour into warmed cups or glasses and dust with a little cinnamon before serving.

CHOCOLATE CHIA OATMEAL COOKIES

MAKES 6 LARGE COOKIES

On the face of it, this recipe really shouldn't work. It makes a wet, sticky batter that doesn't hold a lot of promise. And yet, once it's baked, you're left with a soft, moreish cookie that is perfect with a cold glass of almond milk (my preference) and happens to be pretty darn good for you too—hurrah! Refined sugar-free and packed full of so-called superfoods (chia, cacao, cinnamon, and the rest), these cookies will soon become a go-to recipe in your kitchen too. Personally, I prefer to make them in small batches, otherwise the temptation to consume them all in one sitting is too great, but you could easily double the quantities if you're expecting a crowd. I think they make a particularly good addition to any girls' night in—just add prosecco and it's a party!

generous ¾ cup spelt flour
½ cup rolled oats
1 tablespoon chia seeds
½ teaspoon baking powder
¼ teaspoon sea salt flakes, plus extra
    to decorate
½ teaspoon ground cinnamon, plus extra
    to decorate
1 tablespoon raw cacao powder or cocoa
2 tablespoons agave nectar
2 tablespoons maple syrup

1 tablespoon blackstrap molasses
¼ cup coconut oil, melted
1 tablespoon plant milk (*see* page 9) or water
¼ cup dried cranberries and/or semisweet
    chocolate chips

Coating
3½ oz good-quality semisweet chocolate
    (70% cocoa solids), broken into pieces
1 tablespoon agave nectar
pinch of sea salt flakes

1. Preheat the oven to 400°F and line a baking sheet with parchment paper.
2. In a large bowl, whisk together the flour, oats, chia seeds, baking powder, salt, cinnamon, and cacao until combined.
3. Add the agave nectar, maple syrup, and blackstrap molasses to a small bowl and stir to combine. Make a well in the center of the flour, pour over the coconut oil, agave and maple mixture, and plant milk and gently fold to form a wet, sticky dough.
4. Stir the cranberries and chocolate chips through the dough, then dollop a heaping tablespoon onto the prepared sheet and shape it using 2 spoons. Repeat until all the mixture is used, leaving roughly 2 inches between the cookies to allow for spreading.
5. Bake for 10 to 12 minutes until lightly golden but still nice and soft, then remove from the oven, transfer to a wire rack, and let cool.
6. For the coating, place the chocolate, agave nectar, and salt in a bowl set over a saucepan of lightly simmering water and melt gently, stirring, until completely smooth.
7. Drizzle the melted chocolate mixture over the cooled cookies and finish with a pinch of sea salt and a dusting of cinnamon. Enjoy with almond milk—or prosecco!

CHOCOLATE ORANGE POTS

with a toasted hazelnut & cacao nib crumb

SERVES 4

More like a dessert than a mousse, this rich dessert is only sinful in its sheer simplicity. Silken tofu really comes into its own here and the intense citrus flavor brings back fond memories of that classic British candy, Terry's Chocolate Orange (those sickly sweet segments were such a treat) though it also works well with coffee extract. I can't tell you how many times this easy treat has saved me on the dinner party front; and while the mixture benefits from being chilled, I have frequently served it straight from the blender, dolloped into teeny tumblers, and decorated with the toasted hazelnut and cacao nib crumb. I haven't received any complaints yet.

12 oz silken tofu

3½ oz good-quality semisweet chocolate (70% cocoa solids), broken into pieces

2 tablespoons agave nectar (or 3 tablespoons maple syrup)

1 teaspoon orange extract

pinch of sea salt flakes

orange rind strips, to decorate

Toasted hazelnut and cacao nib crumb

generous ⅓ cup toasted hazelnuts

1 tablespoon cacao nibs

pinch of sea salt flakes

1. Add the tofu to a food processor and blend until smooth.
2. Place the chocolate in a bowl set over a saucepan of lightly simmering water and melt gently, stirring, until completely smooth.
3. Remove the bowl from the heat and let the chocolate cool slightly for 5 minutes, then transfer to the food processor along with the agave nectar, orange extract, and salt. Blend for 5 to 7 minutes until smooth, scraping down the sides with a spatula from time to time.
4. Pour the mixture into 4 ramekins or small glasses. Refrigerate for 2 to 3 hours.
5. To make the crumb, place the toasted hazelnuts, cacao nibs, and salt in a small blender or food processor and pulse together to form a coarse crumblike texture.
6. Sprinkle the crumb over the pots and decorate with a few strips of orange rind just before serving.

MULLED POACHED PEARS

with a silky lemon & thyme cashew cream

SERVES 6

A fabulously easy festive dessert, this exquisite mulled pear dish is truly a thing of beauty. Even if you're not much of a wine drinker, these are worth sampling for their soft-spiced sweetness alone. Served with the delicately infused lemon cashew cream, these pears add a touch of elegance to any gathering—just be sure to blend the cashew cream until silky smooth as there shouldn't be any hint of it having once been a nut. I tend to make both elements in advance, making this recipe a terrific option for a stress-free evening that can be spent socializing rather than sweating in the kitchen. Perfect.

3 cups red wine

4 tablespoons sloe gin (optional, but lovely)

¾ cup packed brown sugar

1 cinnamon stick

2 star anise

1 tablespoon cloves

1 bay leaf

peel of ½ orange

3 large pears (any variety), peeled and cut in half lengthwise with the stalk intact

Lemon & thyme cashew cream

1⅔ cups cashews

1 thyme sprig, plus extra leaves to decorate

7 tablespoons water, plus extra if necessary

grated zest and juice of 1 lemon

1 teaspoon lemon extract

1 heaping tablespoon coconut oil

scant ¼ cup agave nectar

pinch of fine sea salt flakes

1. For the lemon and thyme cream, place the cashews and thyme in a large bowl and cover with freshly boiled water. Set aside to soak and infuse for at least 6 hours, preferably overnight.

2. Drain and rinse the cashews and place in a blender along with the remaining ingredients. Blend for at least 10 minutes until completely smooth, scraping down the sides periodically with a spatula and adding an extra splash of water if necessary. Transfer to a bowl and refrigerate until needed.

3. Place the wine, gin (if using), sugar, cinnamon, star anise, cloves, bay leaf, and orange peel in a large saucepan and bring to a boil, then reduce the heat to a gentle simmer.

4. Gently lower the pear halves into the pan and simmer for 20 minutes, or until soft, inserting a toothpick into the flesh to test. Turn the heat off and let the pears to sit in the warm liquid for another 10 minutes, then carefully remove the pears from the pan and set aside.

5. Bring the poaching liquid to a boil and cook for 10 to 15 minutes, or until reduced to a thick, pourable syrup.

6. To serve, place a dollop or two of cashew cream on the bottom of each dish, top each with a pear half, and drizzle over the reduced mulled wine syrup. Sprinkle over a few extra thyme leaves to finish.

CACAO NIB GRANOLA CLUSTERS

MAKES 6 TO 8 SERVINGS

If you're as obsessed with granola as I am then you'll likely be into this recipe. The ultimate in both cluster and crunch, this granola has the ability to bridge three eating opportunities in one fell swoop —breakfast, dessert, and midmorning/afternoon/early-evening snack. OK, that's clearly more than three, but when something tastes this good, who's counting? With me and my husband regularly reaching into the granola jar, it's sometimes lucky to last a day, but should it make it past the 24-hour mark, I tumble it into my breakfast yogurt or smoothie bowl or use it as a topping for ice cream. The granola might seem spongy when you first remove it from the oven so be sure to let it cool completely before consuming for the full crunch effect.

1 cup rolled oats
¾ cup dry unsweetened coconut
scant ½ cup cacao nibs
1 heaping tablespoon raw cacao powder or cocoa
1 teaspoon ground cinnamon (optional)
8 to 10 medjool dates, pitted
4 dried figs

¼ cup dried cherries or raisins
pinch of sea salt flakes

To serve
dairy-free yogurt, homemade plant milk (*see* page 9), or "Dole Whip" Nice Cream (*see* page 190)

1. Preheat the oven to 340°F. Line a large baking sheet with parchment paper.

2. Place the oats, coconut, and cacao nibs in a food processor and pulse to break up the pieces, then sprinkle over the cacao powder and cinnamon and pulse to combine. Add the dates, figs, cherries, and salt and blend together for 2 to 3 minutes until the mixture forms sticky clumps.

3. Tip the mixture out onto the prepared baking sheet and spread it out so it forms a uniform layer. Transfer to the oven and bake for 15 minutes, then gently turn the clusters using a spatula. Bake for another 10 minutes until the clusters begin to harden and firm.

4. Remove from the oven and let the granola cool completely before transferring to a jar. Serve with dairy-free yogurt, homemade plant milk, or "Dole Whip" nice cream.

SCHOOL CANTEEN
"TRIPLE MINT CHOC" COOKIE SLICE

MAKES 8

This cookie slice conjures up memories of break time, with hordes of schoolgirls streaming toward the canteen in a bid to snaffle any homemade delights that might be on offer. I always made a beeline for the mint chocolate slice, which has lingered on my mind (and taste buds) ever since. Slightly healthier than the original but no less moreish, this is still something of treat and so I reserve it for when friends come over for coffee. It's a perennial gluten-free winner. I'm convinced my younger self would approve.

Base
generous ¾ cup Brazil nuts
scant ½ cup cacao nibs
4 medjool dates, pitted
pinch of sea salt flakes

Filling
1 tablespoon coconut oil
3½ oz good-quality semisweet chocolate, chopped (70% cocoa solids)
2 tablespoons tahini

½ tablespoon agave nectar
1 teaspoon peppermint extract
pinch of sea salt flakes

Topping
2 tablespoons coconut oil, plus extra if necessary
3 tablespoons raw cacao powder or cocoa
1 tablespoon agave nectar
pinch of sea salt flakes

1. Line a 2 lb loaf pan with parchment paper.
2. To make the base, place the Brazil nuts and cacao nibs in a food processor and process to a coarse bread crumblike consistency. Add the medjool dates and salt, and process again until the mixture comes together and is reasonably sticky to the touch.
3. Spread the mixture over the bottom of the pan, pushing it into the edges and pressing it down in an even layer. Transfer to the refrigerator and let chill for around 30 minutes, or until reasonably firm.
4. For the filling, heat the coconut oil in a saucepan over low heat. Add the chocolate to the pan and swirl gently until completely melted, then remove from the heat, add the tahini, agave nectar, peppermint extract, and salt and whisk together vigorously until smooth and glossy. Pour the filling into the loaf pan over the chilled bottom, spreading the mixture to the edges with a spatula, and refrigerate for at least 1 hour, or until set.
5. To make the topping, melt the coconut oil in another saucepan over low to medium heat. Add the cacao powder, agave, and salt and gently stir together until smooth and glossy—if the mixture is looking a little grainy, simply add an extra small piece of coconut oil to loosen it. Pour the topping over the set filling and tip the pan from side to side until it reaches the edges, then return the pan to the refrigerator and let chill for several hours, or ideally overnight.
6. To serve, remove the slice from the refrigerator, using the paper to lift it from the pan, and cut it into small squares. Eat straight away, or keep in an airtight container in the refrigerator for up to 1 week.

PANNA COTTA THREE WAYS

SERVES 2 TO 4

I'm fairly fussy when it comes to dessert. Because I don't indulge in it that often, when I do it has to be a little bit special. These easy panna cottas are just that. You could say that this is simply jelly for grownups, but that shouldn't mean they don't invite some excitement when brought to the table. Perhaps it's their funny wibble (technical term) or maybe it's the ceaseless versatility on the flavor front, but I just can't seem to get enough of them. It also helps that they can be made well in advance, which saves any stress when you have guests. These are my current top three varieties—I love their subtle sweetness and soothing beige hues—but feel free to experiment here yourself. I can't wait to see what you come up with.

1.

VANILLA PANNA COTTA

1 cup water
2 heaping teaspoons agar agar flakes
1 vanilla bean
4 tablespoons superfine sugar
1 cup soy cream
1 teaspoon vanilla extract

Blueberry compote
scant 1¼ cups blueberries
juice of ½ lemon
3 tablespoons sugar

1. Place the water in a small saucepan and sprinkle over the agar agar. Do not stir. Bring to a boil, then simmer over medium heat for 5 to 10 minutes until the agar agar has dissolved.

2. Split the vanilla bean lengthwise and scrape the seeds into the pan. Add the bean to the pan with the sugar and simmer for another 3 to 5 minutes, or until the sugar has dissolved.

3. Whisk in the soy cream and cook gently for 1 to 2 minutes, then take the saucepan off the heat and whisk in the vanilla extract. Set aside and let cool slightly.

4. Pour the mixture into 2 large molds or 4 small glasses. Refrigerate for at least 6 hours, or ideally overnight.

5. To make the compote, place the blueberries in a small saucepan with the lemon juice and sugar. Bring to a gentle simmer and cook for 10 to 15 minutes until the blueberries release their juices and begin to soften. Take off the heat, let cool, and refrigerate until ready to serve.

6. Remove the panna cotta from the refrigerator 5 minutes prior to serving. Place a plate on top of the mold, carefully turn upside down, and shake gently to release the jelly.

7. Serve with the blueberry compote.

2.

COFFEE PANNA COTTA WITH PINE NUT CREAM

1 cup water
2 heaping teaspoons agar agar flakes
3 tablespoons light brown sugar
pinch of sea salt flakes
9 oz carton coconut cream, chilled
(1) 1 oz espresso coffee shot
¼ oz shaved semisweet chocolate (70% cocoa
  solids), to decorate

Pine nut cream
¼ cup pine nuts, soaked and drained
  (see page 8), plus 2 to 3 tablespoons of the
  soaking liquid
2 to 3 tablespoons maple syrup
pinch of sea salt flakes

1. To make the pine nut cream, place the pine nuts in a small blender along with the reserved soaking liquid, maple syrup and salt and blend until completely smooth and thick.

2. Place the water in a small saucepan and sprinkle over the agar agar. Do not stir. Bring to a boil, then simmer over medium heat for 5 to 10 minutes until the agar agar has dissolved.

3. Whisk in the sugar and salt and simmer for another 3 to 5 minutes, or until the sugar has dissolved.

4. Whisk in the coconut cream and espresso and cook gently for 2 to 3 minutes, then take the saucepan off the heat and let cool slightly.

5. Pour the mixture into 2 ramekins or 4 small glasses. Refrigerate for at least 6 hours, or ideally overnight.

6. Remove the panna cotta from the refrigerator 5 minutes prior to serving. Place a plate on top of the mold, carefully turn upside down, and shake gently to release the jelly.

7. Sprinkle over the chocolate shavings to decorate and serve with the pine nut cream.

3.

CHAI PANNA COTTA

1cup water

2 heaping teaspoons agar agar flakes

4 tablespoons coconut palm sugar

1 small cinnamon stick

4 cardamom pods

6 cloves

1 star anise

good grinding of black pepper

pinch of sea salt flakes

¼ teaspoon vanilla powder or 1 teaspoon
vanilla extract

1 cup canned coconut milk

1 tablespoon toasted slivered almonds,
to decorate

Whipped coconut cream

⅔ cup canned coconut cream, chilled

1 tablespoon agave nectar

1. For the whipped coconut cream, place the coconut cream and agave nectar in a mixing bowl and whisk together until light and fluffy. Transfer to the refrigerator and leave for at least 20 minutes to chill and firm.

2. Meanwhile, place the water in a small saucepan and sprinkle over the agar agar. Do not stir. Bring to a boil, then simmer over medium heat for 5 to 10 minutes until the agar agar has dissolved.

3. Whisk in the palm sugar, cinnamon stick, cardamom pods, cloves, star anise, black pepper, salt, and vanilla powder and simmer for 3 to 5 minutes, or until the sugar has dissolved.

4. Stir in the coconut milk and cook gently for 2 to 3 minutes until smooth and silky, then take the saucepan off the heat and let cool slightly.

5. Pour the mixture into 2 ramekins or 4 small glasses. Refrigerate for at least 6 hours, or ideally overnight.

6. Remove the panna cotta from the refrigerator 5 minutes prior to serving. Place a plate on top of the mold, carefully turn upside down, and shake gently to release the jelly.

7. Dollop a spoonful of coconut yogurt on top of each jelly, then sprinkle over the toasted slivered almonds and serve.

GRAPEFRUIT, GIN & SAGE GRANITA

SERVES 4 TO 6

So refreshing and light, granita is the perfect palate cleanser—and when spiked with a decent dose of gin it becomes the perfect aperitif too. With zero skill required to create it (save the scraping, which isn't exactly hard), I find myself experimenting with granita's endless versatility on a semiregular basis. Its soothing, melt-in-your-mouth qualities make it particularly desirable on a piercingly hot summer day. Serve this in chilled glasses and add another splash of gin just before serving for the ultimate adult slushie.

½ cup superfine sugar
grated zest and juice of 1 grapefruit
¼ oz sage, plus extra to decorate
1 cup water
5 tablespoons gin, plus extra to serve

1. Add the sugar, grapefruit zest and juice, sage, and measured water to a saucepan and bring to a boil. Reduce the heat to a simmer and cook for 1 to 2 minutes, or until the sugar has completely dissolved. Remove from the heat and let cool.
2. Strain the cooled sugar syrup through a fine-mesh strainer and add it to a blender along with the gin. Pulse together briefly to combine, then pour into a suitable dish or container and freeze for 1 hour.
3. Remove the granita from the freezer and scrape with a fork to break up the ice crystals, then return to the freezer. Repeat the process every 30 minutes for 2 to 3 hours, or until you have achieved the desired consistency.
4. To serve, spoon the granita into small chilled tumblers or glasses and decorate each with a small sage leaf. Splash over a little extra gin and serve.

PISTACHIO & POMEGRANATE KULFI

SERVES 6 TO 8

I have broken at least two ice-cream machines in my time and so in lieu of having said equipment to hand, I've come to rely on the equally delicious Indian ice cream alternative—kulfi. Simmered and reduced until it has an almost condensed milklike consistency, kulfi has a noticeably denser texture than other frozen desserts and is also very, very sweet. The pistachio paste upon which its magnificence is built is absolutely crucial to its success. For a purer, brighter color, I recommend using skinned pistachios—you can lightly toast them in the oven to make the skins easier to rub off if you can't find them like this. A teaspoon of matcha also goes a long way to boost the color without interfering with the overall flavor. I personally adore the nutty texture here but if you prefer a smoother finish, simply add a touch more water—an extra 7 tablespoons or so—at the blending stage and squeeze the mixture through a nut-milk bag before reducing it on the stove.

generous ¾ cup skinned pistachios
1¼ cups water
1¾ cups canned coconut milk
scant 1 cup raw cane sugar
½ small cinnamon stick
3 to 4 cardamom pods

pinch of pink Himalayan salt
½ tablespoon rose water
½ cup pomegranate seeds, plus extra
   to decorate
handful of dried edible rose petals

1. Line a 1 lb loaf pan with plastic wrap or parchment paper.
2. Add the pistachios and measured water to a blender and blend together for up to 10 minutes until smooth, scraping down the sides from time to time as you go. Transfer to a large pan along with the coconut milk, sugar, cinnamon stick and cardamom pods, and salt, bring to a simmer, and cook for 1 hour until thickened and reduced by at least a third.
3. Remove from the heat and let cool slightly before whisking in the rose water. Set aside for 20 to 30 minutes, or until completely cool.
4. Stir the pomegranate seeds through the cooled mixture, pour it into the prepared loaf pan, and freeze for at least 2 hours, or until set.
5. To remove from the mold, place the pan in a shallow bowl of freshly boiled water for a few seconds. Put a plate on top and carefully turn it over, then tap gently until the kulfi slips out. Remove the parchment paper and let it thaw for 5 minutes before cutting into thick slices and adorning with dried rose petals and a few extra pomegranate seeds.

BAKING
BRILLIANCE

COFFEE CELEBRATION CAKE

SERVES 10 TO 12

Being a coffee fanatic, I can't think of a better way to celebrate than to inject some caffeine into this fun three-tiered cake. With a perfectly nutty crumb, it finishes any grownup gathering with a bang. Vegan baking is usually accompanied by an air of trepidation, but this simple recipe will put those fears to bed. The cake layers won't rise tremendously but once they're stacked and slathered in frosting, everything will begin to make sense. This cake also happens to benefit from being made in advance, giving the flavors ample time to come to the fore—don't worry, it remains surprisingly moist and slices wonderfully too. It's time for afternoon tea.

1 teaspoon balsamic vinegar

scant 1 cup soy milk

scant 2½ cups all-purpose flour

1 tablespoon baking powder

1 teaspoon baking soda

pinch of sea salt flakes

1 teaspoon vanilla powder or extract (optional)

½ cup vegetable shortening

7 tablespoons dairy-free margarine

scant 1 cup packed light brown sugar

4 tablespoons espresso coffee, cooled

1 tablespoon date or maple syrup

1 teaspoon coffee extract

Frosting

¾ cup vegetable shortening

⅔ cup dairy-free margarine

3½ cups confectioners' sugar, plus extra if necessary

1 teaspoon coffee extract

To decorate

2¾ oz shaved semisweet chocolate (70% cocoa solids)

1 cup toasted slivered almonds

1. Preheat the oven to 400°F. Line three 7 inch shallow sponge pans with parchment paper.
2. Combine the balsamic vinegar and soy milk in a bowl and set aside for 5 to 10 minutes to let the mixture curdle.
3. Place the flour, baking powder, baking soda, salt, and vanilla powder, if using, in a mixing bowl and whisk gently to combine.
4. Beat the shortening, margarine, and sugar together in a separate bowl until light and fluffy.
5. Whisk the curdled soy mixture, espresso, date syrup, and coffee extract together until combined, then pour half over the creamed butter and sugar mixture. Add two-thirds of the flour and gently fold to combine, then fold in the remaining liquid and flour mixtures to form a batter.
6. Divide the batter evenly between the prepared cake pans and bake for 25 minutes, or until a cake tester or skewer inserted into the center comes out clean. Set the sponges aside for at least 5 minutes to cool slightly before gently removing from the pan, then transfer to a wire rack and let cool completely.
7. Using an electric whisk or stand mixer, beat the frosting ingredients together until light and fluffy, adding a little more confectioners' sugar if necessary to ensure the frosting holds its shape. Refrigerate until needed.

8. To assemble the cake, dot a cake stand with a little frosting, then lay the first sponge down and press gently to secure. Spread the first layer with the frosting before placing another sponge on top, then repeat until all the layers are sandwiched together. Carefully spread the remaining frosting over the cake, easing it down the sides, and smoothing it with a spatula to coat evenly.

9. Decorate the sides of the cake with shaved chocolate and sprinkle toasted almonds over the top before serving.

ALL-OUT CHOCOLATE HONEYCOMB LOAF

SERVES 8 TO 10

This recipe has a special place in my heart because I made a version of it for my dad's 70th birthday. He had been following a fairly strict plant-based diet (with very little sugar) but for his party he wanted something a little bit special, and I duly delivered. The honeycomb shards make an incredible visual impact and I guarantee people will be practically fighting over who gets to eat the last one. This all-out loaf is a terrifically easy recipe to add to your vegan-baking repertoire.

1 cup all-purpose flour
⅓ cup granulated sugar
⅓ cup raw cacao powder or cocoa
1 teaspoon baking powder
½ teaspoon baking soda
1 banana
3 tablespoons olive oil
½ cup plant milk (*see* page 9)
1 teaspoon vanilla extract

Honeycomb
1 cup superfine sugar
4 tablespoons light corn syrup
1½ teaspoons baking soda

Frosting
3 tablespoons dairy-free margarine
¾ cup conectioners' sugar
1 heaping tablespoon raw cacao powder
or cocoa

1. Preheat the oven to 385°F. Lightly oil a 1 lb loaf pan and line a large baking sheet with parchment paper.
2. Whisk the flour, sugar, cocoa, baking powder, and baking soda together in a large bowl.
3. Mash the banana and whisk together with the oil, plant milk, and vanilla extract until smooth.
4. Make a well in the center of the flour mixture, spoon over the wet ingredients, and gently fold together to form a batter.
5. Spoon the batter into the prepared pan, tapping it firmly on your counter to get rid of any air bubbles. Bake for 30 to 35 minutes, or until lightly golden on top and a cake tester or skewer inserted into the center comes out clean. Remove from the oven and let cool slightly in the pan for at least 5 minutes, then transfer to a wire rack and let cool completely.
6. Meanwhile, make the honeycomb. Mix the sugar and syrup together in a heavy saucepan set over medium to high heat until combined and cook for 2 to 3 minutes until it begins to bubble. Simmer for another 3 to 5 minutes, being sure not to stir as you go, until golden and smooth, then remove from the heat and quickly whisk in the baking soda vigorously until the mixture bubbles before carefully turning it out onto the lined baking sheet. Let cool completely before breaking into shards.
7. For the frosting, beat everything together with an electric whisk or stand mixer until smooth. Refrigerate until needed.
8. When ready to eat, spread the chocolate frosting over the top and sides of the loaf evenly using a spatula and adorn it with the shards of honeycomb. Serve.

BLUEBERRY UPSIDE-DOWN CAKE

with a macadamia cream frosting

SERVES 8 TO 10

Nuts are the cornerstone of my cooking, and their versatility never ceases to amaze me. Here, I've blended them to a flour to give this polenta cake a little more girth. You could use store-bought ground almonds or pistachios, but I think the slightly nubbly texture of home-blended nuts really adds to the overall result. Polenta cakes are often a fine balance of cornmeal (unsurprisingly) and whatever else you choose to pair it with—all-purpose flour works well, but because I wanted to make this a gluten-free affair, I went with a mixture of nuts and gram flour. This way the cake can get by without an official binder (such as flaxseeds or chia) as the small amount of gram flour added ensures that it holds together beautifully and possesses a rather wonderful crumb. Plant-based baking at its natural best.

¾ cup almonds
scant ½ cup pistachios
½ cup cornmeal
scant ¼ cup gram (chickpea) flour
1½ teaspoons baking powder
pinch of sea salt flakes
3½ oz canned pineapple chunks, setting aside the juice (see Macadamia cream)
juice of 1 lemon and zest of 2
3 tablespoons soy yogurt
scant ½ cup maple syrup
5 tablespoons olive oil
scant 2½ cups fresh blueberries
2 tablespoons palm sugar

Macadamia cream

generous ¾ cup macadamias, soaked and drained (*see* page 8)
5 tablespoons reserved pineapple juice
½ teaspoon lemon extract
2 tablespoons agave nectar
1 tablespoon maple syrup
pinch of sea salt flakes

1. Preheat the oven to 385°F. Line an 8 inch cake pan with parchment paper.
2. Place the almonds and pistachios in a food processor and blitz to a fine flour. Transfer to a large mixing bowl and add the cornmeal, gram flour, baking powder, lemon zest and salt. Whisk to combine.
3. Place the pineapple chunks and lemon juice in a food processor and blitz to a coarse puree. Transfer to a mixing bowl and whisk together with the soy yogurt and ⅓ cup of the maple syrup to combine.
4. Make a well in the center of the flour mixture, pour over the oil and the pineapple mixture, and gently fold to form a batter.
5. Cover the bottom of the prepared cake pan with half the blueberries, then pour over the batter and bake for 1¼ hours, or until a cake tester or skewer inserted into the center comes out clean. Remove from the oven and let cool for at least 5 minutes, before removing it from the pan (it's best to turn it upside down for a little while and let it rest for a while before trying this). Transfer to a wire rack and let cool completely.

6. Meanwhile, place the palm sugar in a saucepan along with the remaining blueberries and maple syrup. Bring to a simmer and cook over medium heat for 5 to 10 minutes, or until syrupy. Set aside to cool.

7. To make the macadamia cream, add the macadamias to a food processor and blend to a coarse paste before adding the pineapple juice, lemon extract, agave nectar, maple syrup, and salt. Blend for up to 5 minutes until smooth and fluffy.

8. Once the cake has completely cooled, spoon the macadamia cream over the top and smooth it slightly so it almost meets the edges, then drizzle over the cooled blueberry syrup to finish.

ORANGE BLOSSOM & POPPY SEED SCONE BREAD

SERVES 4

As an Irishwoman, I have sampled my fair share of scone bread—usually in loaf form and almost always made with buttermilk. This version is unapologetically inauthentic, influenced by all three countries in which I have lived—namely England, Ireland, and the United States. A hybrid of sorts, it hopefully takes the best of each nation and combines them to create a light, fluffy bread that can be broken into four sections, slathered in whatever you fancy (I heartily recommend marmalade) and served alongside a cup of tea. The subtle note of orange blossom elevates what is an embarrassingly easy recipe into something really quite elegant. I'm not sure my grandmother would approve, mind, but fortunately everyone I have served it to has loved it.

1 teaspoon cider vinegar

scant ¼ cup soy milk

3 tablespoons agave nectar

grated zest and juice of ½ orange

½ tablespoon orange blossom water

scant 1½ cups all-purpose flour

1 teaspoon baking powder

½ teaspoon baking soda

1 tablespoon poppy seeds

pinch of sea salt flakes

3½ tablespoons dairy-free margarine, refrigerator-cold and cut into cubes

1. Preheat the oven to 425°F.

2. Combine the cider vinegar and soy milk in a bowl and set aside for 5 to 10 minutes to let the mixture curdle.

3. Lightly whisk the soy milk mixture, agave nectar, orange juice, and orange blossom water together in a bowl.

4. Place the flour, baking powder, baking soda, orange zest, poppy seeds, and salt in a large mixing bowl and mix to combine. Add the margarine to the bowl and work it into the flour with your fingertips until the mixture resembles bread crumbs.

5. Make a well in the center of the flour mixture, pour over the wet ingredients, and gently fold together to form a dough.

6. Tip the dough onto a floured baking sheet and shape it into a circle using your hands, then cut it into quarters with a floured knife but don't separate (the pieces will pull apart easily when baked).

7. Bake for 12 to 15 minutes until risen and lightly golden, then remove from the oven and let cool completely before breaking into pieces and serving.

PLUM & ALMOND CAKE

with an Earl Grey pine nut cream

SERVES 6 TO 8

Ground almonds (or "almond meal" if we want to be fancy) are hands-down my favorite thing to use in vegan baking because they lend a cake moistness and density while still retaining an enviable crumb. Genius. As they act almost like a binder, I find I need very little else to ensure my cake turns out, well, "cakey." Of course, this recipe still contains sugar and margarine, so it's pretty far from being a health food, which is precisely why I like it. There's something so comforting about all that creaming, stirring, folding, and waiting; it's easy to see why baking is like therapy to some, as you can't hurry it—or wing it, for that matter. Though the reward for me will always be in the eating, and in that respect this plum and almond affair is just the ticket.

1 teaspoon cider vinegar

⅓ cup soy (or other plant) milk

7 tablespoons dairy-free margarine

¾ cup superfine sugar

scant 1½ cups all-purpose or white spelt flour

½ cup ground almonds

1½ teaspoons baking powder

½ teaspoon baking soda

pinch of sea salt flakes

1 teaspoon almond extract

3 plums, cut into segments

2 tablespoons maple syrup

Earl Grey pine nut cream

¾ cup pine nuts

scant 1 cup freshly brewed Earl Grey tea

1 tablespoon maple syrup

pinch of sea salt flakes

2 to 3 tablespoons water

1. To make the pine nut cream, place the pine nuts in a bowl and cover with the freshly brewed Earl Grey tea. Let soak for 6 hours, or ideally overnight.

2. Preheat the oven to 410°F. Grease and line an 8 inch cake pan.

3. Combine the cider vinegar and soy milk in a bowl and set aside for 5 to 10 minutes to let the mixture curdle.

4. Beat the margarine and sugar together until combined. Gradually sift in the flour, ground almonds, baking powder, baking soda, and salt and whisk together.

5. Add the almond extract to the soy milk and pour into the cake mixture. Fold to form a batter.

6. Pour into the prepared cake pan. Press the plum segments into the batter in concentric circles, overlapping a little if desired. Bake for 60 minutes, covering the top of the cake with parchment paper for the final 15 minutes, or until a cake tester or skewer inserted into the center of the cake comes out clean.

7. Meanwhile, drain the pine nuts, setting aside a tablespoon or so of the soaking liquid and place in a small blender along with the reserved liquid, maple syrup, salt, and water. Blend until completely smooth and thick.

8. Remove the cake from the oven, transfer to a wire rack and brush over the maple syrup. Let cool, then remove from the pan. Slice and serve with a generous dollop of pine nut cream.

EASY WHEATEN LOAF

SERVES 4 TO 6

In my family home there was always a wheaten loaf on the kitchen counter. Granted, it may not have been homemade but nevertheless it was still pretty damn delicious. If you go to Ireland now you'll probably still be offered a slice with just about everything you order—soup, salad, even your main course; it's a bit of a national obsession. This vegan version is bang on the money, despite the absence of buttermilk. Because this recipe is dairy-free I'm using a plant-based baking trick, which is to curdle soy milk with a touch of cider vinegar. You won't believe the difference this makes to the overall texture and flavor of the bread—so much so that my kitchen counter now boasts its very own weekly wheaten loaf. Got to keep those traditions going!

1 teaspoon cider vinegar

1¼ cups soy milk

1⅔ cups rye flour, plus extra for dusting

1⅔ cups all-purpose flour

1 teaspoon baking soda

½ teaspoon pink Himalayan salt

1 tablespoon maple syrup

½ tablespoon blackstrap molasses

1 tablespoon olive oil

½ tablespoon rolled oats

1. Preheat the oven to 425°F. Grease a 1 lb loaf pan and dust the sides with a little flour.
2. Combine the cider vinegar and soy milk in a bowl and set aside for 5 to 10 minutes to let the mixture curdle.
3. Place the flours, baking soda, and salt in a large bowl and whisk together to combine.
4. Whisk the maple syrup, blackstrap molasses, and oil together. Make a well in the center of the flour and pour in the oil mixture along with the soy milk mixture. Use a spatula or fork to work the flour into the liquid in a gradual clockwise motion until it forms a rough dough.
5. Transfer the dough to the pan, spreading the mixture to the sides using a spatula. Sprinkle over the oats and dust with a little rye flour, then bake for 30 minutes, or until the bottom of the loaf sounds hollow when tapped.
6. Remove from the oven, cover with a clean dish towel, and let the bread rest in the pan for 10 minutes before transferring it to a wire rack. Wrap in a clean dish towel and let cool to room temperature, then cut into slices and serve.

VEGAN PAVLOVA

with poached rhubarb & vanilla yogurt

SERVES 6 TO 8

Pavlova—the holy grail of vegan desserts if ever there was one. Who would have thought that chickpea liquid would be the answer to our prayers? A stand mixer or electric mixer is pretty crucial here, and I advise whisking until it's as firm as you can humanly get it before transferring it to the cookie sheet. It's also crucial that you let the meringue cool completely in the oven before removing it. I like to make it a day in advance to avoid any meringue-induced meltdowns, but if you're not serving it immediately, be sure to keep it in an airtight container. If you prefer to make slightly smaller meringues, reduce the cooking time by about 30 minutes. Of course, the topping possibilities are endless but the pale pink of the rhubarb paired with the cool soft white of the yogurt is absolute perfection in my opinion. Enjoy!

7 tablespoons chilled aquafaba (reserved chickpea liquid)

½ teaspoon cream of tartar

scant ⅔ cup superfine sugar

1¾ cups coconut yogurt (*see* page 40)

1 vanilla bean, split lengthwise and seeds scraped

14 oz rhubarb, cut diagonally into 2½ inch chunks

4 tablespoons raw cane sugar

1 strip of lemon peel

1 lemon thyme sprig

1. Preheat the oven to 250°F. Line a large baking sheet with parchment paper.

2. Place the aquafaba in a stand mixer with the whisk attachment added and whisk on medium setting until it becomes thick and frothy. (Alternatively, a large mixing bowl and handheld electric whisk will work equally well, although it may be a little more tasking on the arms.)

3. Add the cream of tartar and whisk on high setting for at least 10 minutes until thick peaks begin to form. Gradually add the superfine sugar, one tablespoon at a time, until it is glossy and thick—this may take anywhere up to 30 minutes but it is crucial the mixture is as stiff as possible, so be patient.

4. Secure the parchment paper on the cookie sheet with a dot of meringue under each corner, then spoon over the meringue and shape it into a rough rectangle using a spatula, spreading it out to almost meet the edges of the sheet. Transfer to the oven and cook for 3½ hours, then turn off the heat and let cool completely in the oven for 6 hours, ideally overnight. Transfer to an airtight container until needed.

5. Whisk the coconut yogurt and vanilla seeds (setting aside the bean) together to combine. Refrigerate until needed.

6. Place the rhubarb in a saucepan along with the cane sugar, lemon peel, thyme, and vanilla bean. Pour over just enough water to cover (scant 1 to 1 cup), bring to a very gentle simmer, and cook for 10 to 12 minutes, or until the rhubarb is just cooked through. Let it cool in the syrup, then refrigerate for several hours, or until needed.

7. To assemble, place the pavlova on a large platter and layer over the coconut yogurt first followed by the chilled rhubarb. Serve immediately and let everyone help themselves.

MINCEMEAT PINWHEELS

MAKES 18

Hands up who loves a cheat recipe! Truthfully, I often cringe at recipes like these but then I find myself turning to them time and again. Ready-made puff pastry is a year-round staple in my kitchen, a godsend for when unexpected guests pop around. I can't tell you how many times I've made these over the years—usually at Christmas, but not always, and it's sometimes worrying how well they are received, the "oohs" and "ahhs" leaving me almost offended on behalf of my other recipes. I like to roll the pastry out a touch before spreading it with an even layer of mincemeat, as it helps it crisp up. Be sure also to secure the ends of the pinwheels as they can have a tendency to unravel … although thankfully that doesn't affect the taste.

1 sheet of vegan ready-made puff pastry, thawed if frozen
½ tablespoon melted coconut oil
1½ teaspoons ground cinnamon
14 oz vegan mincemeat

1 teaspoon water or plant milk (*see page 9*)
generous ⅓ cup slivered almonds
zest of ½ orange
confectioners' sugar, to serve

1. Preheat the oven to 425°F. Line a baking sheet with parchment paper.
2. Roll the pastry out on to a lightly floured counter and brush with the melted coconut oil. Dust the entire sheet with 1 teaspoon of the ground cinnamon and spread the mincemeat over evenly, easing it to the edges using a spatula.
3. Starting from one of the short sides, roll the pastry up tightly into a log. Brush the ends with a little water or plant milk and secure firmly to ensure it doesn't unravel in the oven.
4. Cut the pastry log into ½ inch pieces and place on a prepared baking sheet. Sprinkle over the slivered almonds, dust with the remaining ground cinnamon, and bake for 15 minutes, or until golden.
5. Transfer to a wire rack and let cool for at least 10 minutes. Sprinkle over the orange zest and dust generously with confectioners' sugar to decorate before serving.

STICKY GINGERBREAD BITES

SERVES 10 TO 12

I don't really play favorites when it comes to baking but I must say I have a serious weakness for gingerbread. More like a tray bake, these small squares are sticky sweet and seriously moist—perfect for eating alongside a festive cocktail. I like to pile them up high on a cake stand and either paint them with edible gold leaf or sprinkle them with gold dust. Demure they are not, and all the better for it.

scant 1 cup all-purpose flour
scant ½ cup spelt flour
1 teaspoon baking powder
½ teaspoon baking soda
1 teaspoon ground ginger
½ teaspoon ground cinnamon
½ teaspoon allspice
pinch of sea salt flakes
1 small banana
1 thumb-sized piece of fresh ginger root, peeled and grated
½ cup packed light brown sugar
1 tablespoon blackstrap molasses
1 tablespoon maple syrup
½ cup soy milk (or other plant milk)

1 tablespoon water
1 tablespoon olive oil
½ tablespoon balsamic vinegar

Pomegranate glaze
3 tablespoons pomegranate juice
1 tablespoon satsuma juice
1 teaspoon pomegranate molasses
3 tablespoons agave nectar
1 tablespoon granulated sugar
1 tablespoon dairy-free margarine

To serve
handful of pomegranate seeds
edible gold leaf or dust (optional)

1. Preheat the oven to 385°F. Line a 12 x 8 inch brownie pan with parchment paper.
2. Sift the flours, baking powder, baking soda, spices, and salt into a large bowl.
3. Mash the banana to a smooth puree and transfer to a separate bowl along with the grated ginger, sugar, blackstrap molasses, maple syrup, soy milk, water, oil, and balsamic vinegar. Whisk thoroughly until completely combined.
4. Make a well in the center of the flour, pour in the wet mixture, and fold together gently to form a batter.
5. Pour the batter into the prepared pan and bake for 30 minutes until lightly golden. Remove from the oven and let cool slightly for 10 minutes before removing from the pan and transferring to a wire rack.
6. Meanwhile, add the glaze ingredients to a shallow skillet. Bring to a boil, then reduce the heat to a simmer and cook for 10 to 15 minutes until reduced, thickened, and syrupy.
7. While the bread is still warm, pour or brush over the glaze, covering it entirely. Sprinkle over a generous handful of pomegranate seeds and for a final, festive flourish, paint on some edible gold leaf or sprinkle over a little gold dust, if you fancy. Let cool completely before cutting into bite-sized squares.

CAKEY BAKED DOUGHNUTS

with a vibrant cashew frosting

MAKES 6 DOUGHNUTS

These doughnuts are a cinch to make and taste just as good as the real thing. I rarely go in for foodie fads but my mini-doughnut pan gets so much use and I always have fun experimenting with frostings and toppings. A glaze or drizzle works fine here—although they are good enough without—but nothing beats a generous smear of homemade cashew frosting to elevate a doughnut to greater heights. Vegan food colorings are available pretty much everywhere now (just check the label) and I find pale shades work best here, providing a gorgeous contrast to the delicate freeze-dried strawberries.

1 teaspoon cider vinegar

⅔ cup soy milk

1 tablespoon melted coconut oil

½ cup unrefined superfine sugar

1 teaspoon vanilla extract

generous ¾ cup all-purpose flour

½ cup coconut flour

1 teaspoon baking powder

½ teaspoon baking soda

pinch of sea salt flakes

1 heaping tablespoon freeze-dried
    strawberries, to decorate

Frosting

¾ cup cashews, soaked and drained
    (*see page 8*)

⅓ cup agave nectar

grated zest and juice of ½ lemon

½ tablespoon coconut oil

1 teaspoon vanilla extract

2 tablespoons water

a selection of 3 vegan food colorings

1. Begin by making the frosting. Place all the ingredients, except your choice of food colorings, in a high-speed blender and blend until completely smooth, scraping down the sides from time to time. Refrigerate for at least 1 hour.

2. Preheat the oven to 400°F. Lightly grease a mini-doughnut pan.

3. Combine the cider vinegar and soy milk in a bowl and set aside for 5 to 10 minutes to let the mixture curdle. Once curdled, add the coconut oil, sugar, vanilla extract, and 1 tablespoon of water and whisk until frothy.

4. Place the flours, baking powder, baking soda, and salt in a large mixing bowl and whisk lightly to combine.

5. Make a well in the center of the flour, add the liquid, and fold gently to form a wet dough.

6. Transfer the dough to a pastry bag and pipe it into the prepared doughnut pan to fill the molds, smoothing them with the back of a spoon. Bake for 12 minutes, or until lightly golden, then transfer to a wire rack to cool for 1 to 2 minutes before removing from the pan and letting cool completely.

7. Remove the frosting from the refrigerator and divide it between 3 mixing bowls. Add 1 teaspoon of food coloring to each bowl and whisk vigorously with an electric whisk until it is light and fluffy.

8. Generously spread the frosting over the doughnuts and sprinkle over the strawberries to finish.

RED PEPPER & HUMMUS MUFFINS

MAKES 6 LARGE MUFFINS

I have been keeping this muffin recipe close to my chest for years, with many versions having been consumed while I perfected it. I think it was worth the wait. The inclusion of hummus was the breakthrough—it not only binds everything together but gives these muffins a real depth of flavor. You could make your own but I actually find that store-bought hummus is best in this particular instance. While I've gone for strong white flour, spelt would also be stellar. And don't be afraid of overfilling your pan—the bigger the muffin-top, the better.

1 teaspoon cider vinegar
⅓ cup soy milk
2 tablespoons olive oil
1 red bell pepper, cored, seeded, and diced
2 scallions, sliced
1¼ cups strong white flour
1 teaspoon baking powder

½ teaspoon baking soda
½ teaspoon sea salt flakes
¼ teaspoon black pepper
½ cup chopped cilantro
3 tablespoons hummus
1 tablespoon maple syrup

1. Preheat the oven to 400°F. Line a 6-hole muffin tray with muffin cups or strips of parchment paper.
2. Combine the cider vinegar and soy milk in a bowl and set aside for 5 to 10 minutes to let the mixture curdle.
3. Heat 1 tablespoon of the olive oil in a skillet over medium heat. Add the pepper and scallions, season, and sauté until just beginning to soften. Remove from the heat and set aside until needed.
4. Place the flour, baking powder, baking soda, salt, pepper, and chopped cilantro in a large bowl and whisk to combine.
5. In a separate bowl, whisk the hummus, maple syrup, soy milk mixture, and remaining 1 tablespoon of olive oil together until smooth.
6. Make a well in the center of the flour. Add the hummus mixture together with the sautéed peppers and scallions and gently fold together.
7. Divide the batter evenly between the muffin holes and bake for 20 minutes until risen and lightly golden.
8. Transfer the tray to a wire rack and let the muffins cool slightly before easing them from the pan. Let cool completely, then transfer the muffins to an airtight container and enjoy when you like (they will keep for up to 1 week).

PUMPKIN MUFFINS

MAKES 6 LARGE MUFFINS

As soon as fall makes an appearance I unleash my pumpkin-baking prowess. These are months I relish and I always feel the need to make the most of the season. Right up until Thanksgiving (a tradition we've adopted since living in Chicago) my house is filled with the scents of cinnamon and nutmeg, usually emanating from some sort of baked good. These simple pumpkin muffins are surprisingly versatile and can be enjoyed in a multitude of ways: if eating them hot like this, I prefer to leave them unglazed and spread them with coconut or dairy-free butter, though they are also great drizzled with a sweetened version of my "Goes-with-Everything" Tahini Sauce (*see* page 151). I also like to stir fruit through the batter before baking—apples are good, as are cranberries but I think my favorite is pear. Have a play around, see what you like best and be sure to make the most of those pumpkins.

1 small to medium-sized pumpkin, halved and seeds removed	pinch of sea salt flakes
scant 1½ cups spelt flour	3 tablespoons olive oil
⅓ cup superfine or light brown sugar	1 tablespoon maple syrup
2 teaspoons baking powder	½ tablespoon blackstrap molasses
1 teaspoon ground cinnamon	1 teaspoon vanilla extract
¼ teaspoon ground ginger	4 tablespoons soy milk
¼ teaspoon freshly grated nutmeg	1 tablespoon water
¼ teaspoon pumpkin pie spice	coconut butter or dairy-free margarine, to serve

1. Preheat the oven to 425°F.
2. Arrange the pumpkin halves skin-side down on a baking sheet, pour over ⅔ cup water (this will prevent it from sticking to the bottom and will help it steam slightly) and roast for 1 hour, or until the skin is easily pierced with a sharp knife. Remove from the oven, turn the pumpkin halves over, and let cool for 10 to 15 minutes, then scoop out the soft flesh and let cool completely before transferring to a blender and blending to a fine puree. Transfer to an airtight container and set aside until needed.
3. Reduce the oven temperature to 400°F and grease and line a 6-hole muffin pan with muffin cups or strips of parchment paper.
4. Whisk the spelt flour, sugar, baking powder, spices, and salt together in a large bowl.
5. In a separate bowl, combine 3½ oz of the pumpkin flesh together with the olive oil, maple syrup, blackstrap molasses, vanilla extract, soy milk, and measured water.
6. Make a well in the center of the flour, pour in the pumpkin mix, and gently fold until just combined, ensuring not to overwork the batter.
7. Divide the batter evenly between the muffin holes and bake for 20 to 25 minutes until risen and lightly golden. Serve hot with coconut butter or dairy-free margarine or let cool and keep for up to 1 week in an airtight container.

INDEX

A heartfelt thank you to Octopus for the incredible support, guidance and endless positivity … it's been a joy from beginning to end. Special thanks goes to Alison for the opportunity to join the Octopus family – I couldn't hope for a better editor. Huge thanks also goes to Jonathan for his incredible artistic prowess in bringing this whole beautiful book together, Alex for her beady (and much needed) grammatical eye, and copy editor extraordinaire Simon. Dream team doesn't even cover it.

To Chris, my agent, thanks for believing in me and helping this little cookbook author have a bit more faith in herself.

To the fab three (Danielle, Frankie and Ted) who made the food look so darn gorgeous, a colossal high five … you brought my food to life in a way I couldn't imagine, your collective creativity was boundless and inspiring.

Thanks to the talented foodie assistants Sophie McKinnon and Charlotte O'Connell … really lovely working with you, your calming presence was appreciated.

Thank you to Anna Šebestová for her stunning illustrations that complement the design and food so wonderfully.

To my mother, Marie, for helping me bring this book to fruition despite the difficult circumstances … know that Dad's presence was with me the entire time, cheering me along. To my sister, friend and number one fan, Mairead, you have been a rock and a constant source of optimism. Ronan, you joined our family during our most trying year …, grateful to have you in our lives. And to my everything, my love, my Jason – your unending confidence in my abilities has made all of this possible, so thank you.

An Hachette UK Company
www.hachette.co.uk

First published in Great Britain in 2018 by Mitchell Beazley, a division of Octopus Publishing Group Ltd
Carmelite House, 50 Victoria Embankment, London EC4Y 0DZ
www.octopusbooks.co.uk
www.octopusbooksusa.com

Text copyright © Áine Carlin 2018
Design, illustrations & photography © Octopus Publishing Group Ltd 2018

Distributed in the US by Hachette Book Group
1290 Avenue of the Americas, 4th and 5th Floors, New York, NY 10104

Distributed in Canada by Canadian Manda Group
664 Annette Street, Toronto, Ontario, Canada M6S 2C8

ISBN 978 1 78472 412 2

A CIP catalogue record for this book is available from the British Library.

Printed and bound in China

10 9 8 7 6 5 4 3 2 1

Publisher	Alison Starling
Creative Director	Jonathan Christie
Senior Editor	Alex Stetter
Senior Production Manager	Katherine Hockley
Copy Editor	Simon Davis
Photography	Danielle Wood
Home Economist and Stylist	Frankie Unsworth
Illustrations	Anna Šebestová

ACKNOWLEDGMENTS